Report on the Development of Household Finance in Rural China (2014)

Li Gan · Zhichao Yin · Jijun Tan

Report on the Development of Household Finance in Rural China (2014)

Springer

Li Gan
Southwestern University of Finance and Economics
Chengdu, Sichuan
China

Jijun Tan
Southwestern University of Finance and Economics
Chengdu, Sichuan
China

Zhichao Yin
Southwestern University of Finance and Economics
Chengdu, Sichuan
China

ISBN 978-981-10-0408-7 ISBN 978-981-10-0409-4 (eBook)
DOI 10.1007/978-981-10-0409-4

Library of Congress Control Number: 2016932317

Printed on acid-free paper

This Springer imprint is published by SpringerNature
The registered company is Springer Science+Business Media Singapore Pte Ltd.

Contents

Chapter 1
Basic Condition of Rural Households

1.1 Survey Design

1.1.1 A Brief Introduction to the Survey

Southwestern University of Finance and Economics (SWUFE) launched the China Household Finance Survey (CHFS) in 2009 and established the Survey and Research Center for China Household Finance (hereafter referred to as "the Center") in 2011. The nationwide door-to-door survey, carried out in every other year, aims at collecting micro-level information about household finances. The survey content includes real estate assets and financial assets, debts and credit constraints, income, consumptions, social security and insurance, intergenerational transfer payments, population demographics, employment and related information like payment habits. And the micro-level household financial data has contributed to economic academic research and policy making with its consistently careful tracking and portrayal of finance. The China Household Finance Survey has details about many aspects, and CHFS has built a fundamental micro-level database for society to share and study together.

The Center carried out its first survey in 2011 and released the data one year later, having great impact on society. In China, research on household finance has not started until recently. Therefore, the findings of CHFS have just filled the void in academic research on this area. The research significance has been beyond the academic circle and produced widespread social benefits. The date published by the Center has garnered great interest in academic circle and led to a series of research achievements. As for social benefits, the Center has been engaging in studying and discussing China's major policy issues like real estate market regulation, income distribution, economic transition, urbanization, and etc.

Agricultural Bank of China is one of the major suppliers of comprehensive financial service in China. With overall business types, vast distribution network

L. Gan et al., *Report on the Development of Household Finance in Rural China (2014)*, DOI 10.1007/978-981-10-0409-4_1

and advanced technological platform, it provides the clients with financial services in various areas including commercial banking, investment banking, fund management, financial lease, and life insurance, etc. It has already become a first-class and modern commercial bank that is oriented to agriculture, involved in urban-rural collaborative development and international growth and offering diversified services. It ranked 64th in Fortune's list of Global Top 500 in 2013 and 5th in *The Banker*'s list of Global Top 1000 Banks by right of tier one capital in 2012. Serving the agricultural development is not only the responsibility of Agricultural Bank of China, the mainstay of China's rural finance, but also the strategic choice for its development. Targeting at the market of agriculture, farmers and rural area, the Bank takes the reform of its agricultural finance sector as the mechanism guarantee, and attaches great importance to "121 Project (collaborative development plan of one city, two regions and a hundred gardens)", "Thousand and Hundred Project (renovating a thousand villages among which one hundred are set to be models)", "Gold Ear Project (project benefiting rural clients with gold ear cards)" and "County Level Retail Business Promotion Project". By enhancing the preferential allocation of resources, the channel construction, production innovation, client management and risk regulation, the Bank's agricultural finance service has continuously improved. It has attached great importance to the cutting-edge issues of rural finance and continuously enhanced the communication with experts in various fields. In August, 2013, the Bank signed a cooperative agreement on China Household Finance Survey with Southwestern University of Finance and Economics. Thus the bank assists the survey by taking the advantage of its wide-spreading branches, lowering the refusal rate by a large scale. Meanwhile, the two parties fully explore the first hand data of rural household finance, and co-research the subjects including rural household's credit demand and availability, rural household's financial risk and literacy and private lending, etc. The research, which is of great importance both theoretically and practically, has not only provided the nation's agricultural policy-making with quantitative reference, but also supported the agricultural financial service of financial organizations.

1.1.2 The Sampling Process

1.1.2.1 Sampling Summary

In order to ensure the randomness and representativeness of the sample, and realize CHFS's goal to research on household asset allocation, consumption, savings, etc., sampling design has to meet the following four requirements: first, the proportion of samples collected from rich areas is relatively large; second, the proportion of samples from urban areas is relatively large; third, the areas of samples are evenly distributed geographically; fourth, to economize the cost as much as possible. Generally, the project's sampling is carried out in three stages, in each stage collecting samples from different level, and adopts PPS method. In the first stage, counties (cities) nationwide are collected as samples; in the second stage residents' committees and village committees of sampled counties and cities are collected; in the third stage households are collected in the sampled committees. In each stage the sampling is also carried out with PPS method with population or the number of households in each sampled area as the weight. There were 8348 households surveyed in the first round and 28,000 for the second time.

From July to August, 2011, the Survey and Research Center for China Household Finance conducted the survey for the first time. The primary sampling units were taken from 2585 counties (districts and county-level cities) all over the country except Tibet, Xinjiang, Inner Mongolia, Hong Kong, Macao, and Taiwan. In the first stage of sampling, we divided the primary sampling units into 10 strata according to GDP per capita and selected 8 counties from each level, totaling 80 counties covering 25 provinces in China. The village committee and neighborhood committee ratio in each sampled county (district or county-level city) is based on the proportion of non-agricultural population, and the number of village committee and neighborhood committee in total is always 4. For each sampled village/neighborhood committee, the higher the house price is, the more households are surveyed, and thus in each committee there are 20–50 households being surveyed. We interviewed the family members who meet the survey requirements thus to guarantee the samples' nationwide representativeness. The survey in first two stages was carried out in paper work with the help of demographic statistics, and the final stage sampling was conducted onsite.

In 2013, the Center expanded its sampling quantity. The primary sampling unit (PSU) covered cities and counties all over the country excluding Tibet, Xinjiang, Hong Kong, Macao, and Taiwan. While the data is nationally representative, the sampling design also guaranteed its representativeness at provincial level.

During the first stage of sampling, all counties (districts and county-level cities) in each province were listed according to their GDP per capita, and then sampled symmetrically on the basis of the per capita GDP in 2011. For example, if the county/county-level city sampled ranked 15th in 100 of a province in 2011, the new sample of 2013 would have to be symmetrically the 85th one in terms of GDP per capita. By this method, if the number of samples of a province were too few to be provincially representative, we adopted the PPS sampling method to increase samples (see specific implementation). For the newly sampled three provinces Ningxia, Inner Mongolia, and Fujian, we also used the Probability Proportional Sample (PPS) method. Specifically, a province's counties (districts and county-level cities), ranked by per capita GDP, were dealt with systematic sampling and weighted by population. The sampling ultimately got 262 cities and counties across 29 provinces including 182 new ones.

1.1.2.2 Specific Operations

1. Household Mapping
   Onsite sampling is based on mapping the residential areas and collecting lists of households. The precision of the map directly affects the quality of the last stage of sampling.
   CHFS has developed a geographic information sampling system using remote sensing, GPS, and GIS (3G) to collect the geographic information of the targeted areas. The fine digital imagery and vector maps used in mapping come from the Institute of Geographic Information in the Chinese Academy of Sciences. When in the field, our mapping technicians use an electronic measuring instrument and a GPS system to collect accurate electronic data which is automatically transferred to computers to create high-quality vector maps. We also consider potential post-collection changes of the geographic data and manually check and record any changes that appear at following stages. This ensures that the geographic information in the system's virtual world matches the one in real world. The system not only allows our mapping technicians to draw residential household locations directly onto the electronic map but also stores relevant household location information which is used for the last stage of sampling. This innovation improves efficiency, decreases potential mapping and sampling errors, and helps protect the privacy of household information. The working procedure is illustrated in Fig. 1.1.
2. Selecting Households
   We use equal-space sampling to draw households from the household list collected during the previous mapping stage.
   First, we calculate the sampling interval, i.e., the number of households from which one is chosen, using the following formula:

$$\begin{aligned}\text{Sampling interval} = {} & \text{total number of households in the community} \\ & /\text{number of households to be selected} \\ & (\text{rounded up to the closest integer}).\end{aligned}$$

Fig. 1.1 Mapping process

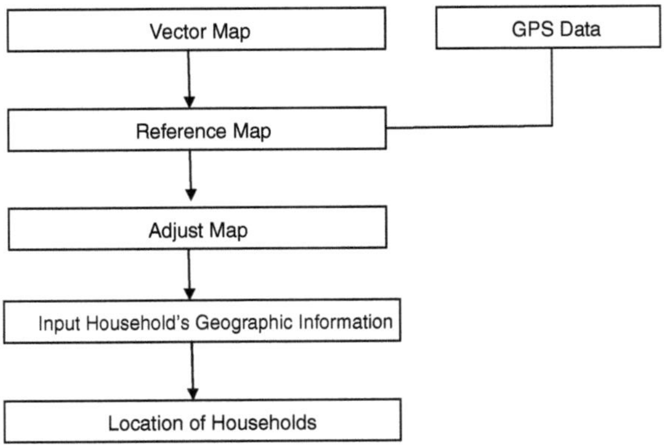

For example, if we plan to draw 30 households from the 100 households of the residential committee/village, we get 100/30 = 3.33. Then the sampling interval is 4.

Second, the random starting point is decided by the final digit of the clock time when the procedure is carried out. For example, if the clock time is 15:34, then 4 is the starting point.

Third, we draw the households. The first selected household is the one whose position on the list corresponds to the random starting point. Using the above example again, if 4 is the starting point and 4 is the sampling interval, the 4th household on the list is the first one chosen in the sample, followed by the 8th, 12th, 16th, 20th, and so on until all 30 households are drawn.

In the sample, households are defined as follows: a household can be divided into large households and single-person households. Multi-person households can have a husband and wife, parents, children, siblings, etc., with members who can be interviewed directly. Single-person households are divided based on the following two conditions: there are no other household members that can be interviewed directly; or, if there are household members in other places but they are economically independent of each other, then other household members are not counted as household members. Moreover, the household must have at least one person who has Chinese nationality and has been living in that region for at least six months. In general, the principle to identify a household is that either the family members share revenues or expenses.

3. Weighted Summary

   According to our sampling design, since each household is drawn with different probabilities, the number of members per Chinese household is different. In general, inferences are required to accurately reflect the number of households per sample and households are represented by adjusting the weights to make correct inferences about the population. All calculations for the China Household Finance Survey sample weights have been adjusted. Sampling weights are calculated as follows, respectively: based on a survey sample of each stage of the counties have been drawn in the probability P1, probability of that community (village) being selected for the survey in their respective districts to be P2, and the survey sample in their respective communities (villages) are drawn probability P3, respectively, to calculate the weight of the three-stage sampling weights: W1 = 1/P1, W2 = 1/P2, W3 = 1/P3, and finally to obtain the weight of the sample, W = W1 × W2 × W3.

1.1.3 Data Collection

1.1.3.1 Introduction to the CAPI and CATI Operating Systems

The CHFS project draws on the sophisticated and internationally-recognized Computer-Assisted Interviewing (CAPI) framework and design concept, developed with independent intellectual property rights and related platform for the interview management system. Through this system, we are able to fully utilize the computer as a means of conducting electronic interviews. In this way, we can effectively reduce non-sampling errors caused by human factors, such as the preset range problems, data entry errors, and errors in logic. CAPI can better meet data acquisition confidentiality and real-time requirements, which can significantly improve the quality of survey data.

1.1.3.2 Interviewer Selection and Training

The CHFS interviewers are mainly undergraduate and graduate students from SWUFE. They are well-versed in economics, thoroughly understand the questionnaire, and can effectively communicate with respondents to explain the questionnaire. All CHFS interviewers received the following training before going into the field.

First, they were trained in interviewing skills. The training included how to identify qualified interviewees and build trust; how to ask and explain questions in a precise and neutral way; how to deal with emergent issues during an interview; and how to save and transmit data while preserving the confidentiality of the respondents' information.

Second, the interviewers were given training to ensure they understood the questionnaire. We divided the interviewers into small groups, familiarized them with the questions, and ensured that each of them understood the questions. We also employed PPT, video clips, and other multimedia technology to make the process exciting and engaging. Interviewers conducted mock interviews in the classroom, observed one another's performances, and discussed better ways to perform their tasks.

Third, they were trained in the CAPI (Computer-Assisted Personal Interviewing) system and the corresponding survey management system. Each interviewer was given a laptop with both the CAPI system and the management system pre-installed. An appropriate amount of time was spent teaching the interviewers to become efficient users of both the equipment and the software. They were also trained to make remarks and use various shortcuts during interviews.

Fourth, the interviewers were trained to conduct trial interviews in the field. In addition to classroom training, we accompanied the trainees to conduct trial interviews in surrounding neighborhoods to test their acquisition of interview skills and questionnaire content. They were then each given extensive and detailed feedback to help them further improve their skills.

In summary, our 232 mapping technicians went through five rounds of training averaging 42 h in total. Additionally, we trained 343 interviewers, each of whom received an average of 80 h of training. Each trainee was evaluated based on rigorous standards at the end of training. Unqualified trainees were asked to repeat the training or face dismissal.

The field auditors were mainly doctoral students at SWUFE. Since they shouldered the important responsibilities of managing interviewers and the fieldwork, each field auditor received over 30 h of rigorous and extensive training. All auditors became proficient users of the interview monitoring system, the interview assignment system, and the CAPI system.

The rigorous training and evaluation procedures produced first-rate field auditors and interviewers, thus building a solid foundation for collecting high-quality data.

1.1.4 Refusal Rate

1.1.4.1 Distribution of the Refusal Rate

CHFS uses two types of statistical standards for its refusal rate. There were standard rates for the refusal rate's broad range. Refusals included households that refused to be interviewed, empty households, and households that did not meet the conditions to be sample households. The first interview refusal rate was calculated as follows:

Refusal Rate 1 = (households that refuse to be interviewed + empty households + households that do not meet conditions) ÷ (households that refuse to be interviewed + empty households + households that do not meet conditions + interviewed households)

The second standard is the diameter of the refusal rate, so the sample's interview refusal rate includes only households refusing to be interviewed. The calculation for the second interview refusal rate is:

Refusal Rate 2 = refusal rate ÷ (households that refuse to be interviewed + interviewed households)

Table 1.1 has the statistics of the distribution of the two standards' 2011 survey refusal rates. In both computed diameters, none of the overall refusal rates is greater than 20 %. This was thanks to community and village respondents and their professionalism and active cooperation with the interviewers. From Table 1.1 we discover that the overall refusal rate is not high but there is a big difference between

Table 1.1 Differences in the urban and rural refusal rates

	Overall (%)	Urban (%)	Rural (%)
Refusal rate 1	18.4	22.6	8.4
Refusal rate 2	11.6	16.5	3.2

Table 1.2 Distribution of the 2011 CHFS refusal rate

	Overall (%)	Eastern region (%)	Central region (%)	Western region (%)
Refusal rate 1	18.4	20.7	16.1	14.4
Refusal rate 2	11.6	15.5	9.7	4.4

the urban and rural areas. For example, for refusal rate 2, the refusal rate of urban areas (16.5 %) is five times greater than the refusal rate in rural areas (3.2 %).

Table 1.2 shows the refusal rate distributed even further, into eastern, western, and central regions. It is easily discovered that regardless of whether it is refusal rate 1 or refusal rate 2, or whether it is the eastern, western, or central region (with the regions mentioned above having respectively decreasing refusal rates), the higher a region's level of economic development, the lower the respondents' enthusiasm to be interviewed. Most of the households surveyed in the east were in urban areas and the maximum for the two refusal rates in the urban areas was 15.5 %, far higher than 4.4 and 9.7 % in the western and central regions, respectively. As the final survey extracts eastern, western, and central samples of 32:27:21 and a survey design of multiple urban communities, this makes the refusal rates of the western and central areas lower than overall refusal rate (18.4 or 11.6 %). In order to ensure the quality of the survey and a low refusal rate, CHFS invested a great deal of manpower and resources into the communities that were interviewed.

In order to gain a deeper understanding of CHFS' refusal rate, Table 1.3 described the grouping of different interview refusal rates in 320 communities' distributions of refusal rates from CHFS 2011. As shown in Table 1.3, for the standard refusal rate 2, there were 191 communities with a refusal rate of 0, meaning that all the drafted communities were interviewed. Among them, there were 53 urban communities and 138 rural communities. In urban communities, the

Table 1.3 Distribution of the 2011 CHFS community refusal rates

Standard refusal rate	Region	Community data			
		0 %	0–20 %	20–40 %	Greater than 40 %
Refusal rate 1	Overall	88	137	79	16
	Urban	16	68	63	14
	Rural	72	69	16	2
	Eastern	23	60	38	7
	Central	37	41	23	7
	Western	18	36	18	2
Refusal rate 2	Overall	191	89	30	10
	Urban	53	75	26	7
	Rural	138	14	4	3
	Eastern	69	39	13	7
	Central	61	33	11	3
	Western	61	17	6	0

Chart 1.1 2011 CHFS distribution of refusal rates in urban and rural areas

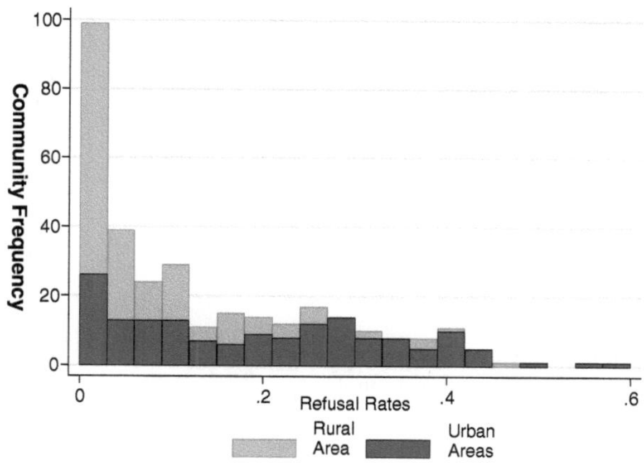

refusal rates were largely concentrated in the 0–20 % range, with only seven communities having a refusal rate higher than 40 %; in rural areas 138 communities had a refusal rate of 0 and only 21 communities had a refusal rate that was not 0. Moreover, while communities in the eastern and central regions had relatively closer refusal rates, communities in the western region had a substantially larger number of refusal rates higher than 40 %.

Chart 1.1 depicts a histogram with further distribution of the interview refusal rates in 320 communities. The figure on the horizontal axis represents the different levels of refusal rates. The vertical axis represents the corresponding refusal rate at the community level. The light areas of the figure represent the distribution of the overall refusal rate under the particular amount of communities' refusal rates; the dark regions are data from urban communities. Table 1.3 is consistent with the conclusion that the majority of refusal rates are concentrated in the 20 % range while the number of communities with a refusal rate higher than 40 % is very low and mainly consists of urban communities.

1.1.4.2 How the Refusal Rate Compares Longitudinally

Practice has proven that through the survey's continuous development, CHFS' influence has grown and, compared to 2011, the overall 2013 CHFS refusal rate decreased. As shown in Table 1.4, in 2013, regardless of whether it was overall or for urban and rural areas, the refusal rate fell. This was especially true in rural areas where the refusal rate was less than 1 %, meaning that there was a high success rate with rural households.

Meanwhile, the 2013 CHFS sample is included in Table 1.5 with received samples from the 2011 household survey. The households that had been interviewed in 2011 also participated in the 2013 survey had a sample refusal rate of less than half. As a side note, as the project progressed, there was an increase in social recognition and acceptance of financial surveys of Chinese households, improving the quality of the data and providing advantageous support.

Table 1.4 How CHFS' refusal rate compares longitudinally

Timeframe	Refusal rate (%)	
2011	Overall	11.6
	Urban	16.5
	Rural	3.2
2013	Overall	10.9
	Urban	15.4
	Rural	0.9

Table 1.5 Comparison of the old and new samples' refusal rates

Sample set	2013 (%)	
Old samples	Overall	5.4
	Urban	8.2
	Rural	0.7
New samples	Overall	12.6
	Urban	17.4
	Rural	0.9

1.2 Data Quality Control

1.2.1 Process of Controlling the Quality of the Interviews

In addition to using computer-assisted personal interviewing (CAPI), the project also designed a more comprehensive quality assurance system in order to reduce the number of problems caused by human error, including.

1.2.1.1 Strict Management of the Samples

Although interviewed samples are managed on the computer, the interviewer cannot reduce the difficulties of interviewing and finding replacement samples to ensure the maximum representativeness and randomness for the sample. Interviews must be refused or unanswered six times before the interviewer can go about overseeing a replacement sample. Even after personally confirming the replacement sample, it may not be possible to replace the sample. The CAPI system, accompanied with a smooth management system, is a key element for the work to proceed smoothly.

Main features of the system include sample building, sample distribution, sample development, sample maintenance, sample tracking, interviewing, supervision and management, and the dissemination and implementation of verified samples. The specific process is as follows:

1. Build the sample data based on the sampling results obtained during the third stage of sampling (housing ID number, map drafting ID number, information about housing address, etc.).
2. The interviewers, field supervisors, and other data personnel arrive and establish relationship with their corresponding interviewers or supervisors.
3. According to the sample target goals, rules and regulations provided to the samples are disbursed to supervisors and interviewers.
4. Each client has his or her data returned in real time, in accordance with the established rules for presenting data.

Parts of the collected data include: the timeframe for receiving sample data, the timeframe for delivering sample data, and changing the sample's data history.

1.2.1.2 Details of the Interview Management System

There are four main functions of the interview management system: first, the sample data receives data management and issues a tracking system; second, respondent households are contacted to collect their contact information; third, survey data collection is conducted through a Blaise questionnaire; fourth, the collected data is returned in a timely manner.

Data acquired in this part includes: survey data, access to contact information and data (time contacted, outcome of making contact, manner of making contact, the environment where contact was made, appointment time, manner of the appointment, etc.), interviewers' behavioral data (time it took to answer, intervals between answers, sequence of the answers, keyboard and mouse operations to record, etc.), the time it took for the sample data to be returned, etc.

1.2.1.3 Timely Return of Data

In the above synchronized data, VPN client users access data through the server under the premise of a stable link of communication. They use the host server and distribute the work in order to synchronize data with a subscription model to satisfy supporting staff's access to continued real-time analysis and verify the quality requirements.

1.2.2 Data Inspection

During the interview contact phase, we ask interviewers for detailed information about each round of contact, such as the time of knocking on the door, accompanying persons, respondents' reactions, etc. Such information helps with analysis of the reasons for being refused interviews, providing additional response options for the interviewers, and preventing interviewers from easily replacing samples.

With CAPI's data logging system, interviewers use mouse and keyboard operations to record al interviews, and all interviewers faithfully record detailed behavioral data during the interview. As area network conditions allow, this recording can be promptly returned to the project server, enabling near real-time monitoring. Specific tasks include:

1. *Telephone interviews*: All households with a telephone receive a follow-up interview to confirm whether they have received access.
2. *Inspection of recordings*: There is access to the recordings all the way to playing back recordings for verification.
3. *Analysis of the "paradata" (behavioral data)*: This is to inspect and statistically analyze the collected behavioral data.

1.3 Household Demographics

1.3.1 Household Composition

In 2013, CHFS collected a total of approximately 28,000 valid household samples. The sample size included 98,045 individuals with an average household size of 3.5 people. The average urban and rural households have 3.2 people and 4 people, respectively. There were 2754 households consisting of one person, accounting for 9.9 % of the total sample; 8492 households consisted of 2 people, accounting for 30.6 % of the total sample; 7443 households had three people, accounting for 26.8 % of the total sample; 4361 households consisted of four people, accounting for 15.7 % of the total sample; 2810 households had five people, accounting for 10.1 % of the sample; and 1278 households consisted of six people, accounting for 4.6 % of the sample. In addition, there are 605 households consisting of more than six people, accounting for 2.2 % of the sample. The component ratios of different household sizes are shown in Chart 1.2.

1.3.2 Gender Structure

The basic descriptive statistics are shown in Table 1.6; there are 49,903 males and 48,141 females listed and the sex ratio is 103.7:100. There is a large disparity in the sex ratio between urban and rural areas, with urban areas having a male-to-female sex ratio of 100.2:100 and rural areas having a sex ratio of 109.5:100.

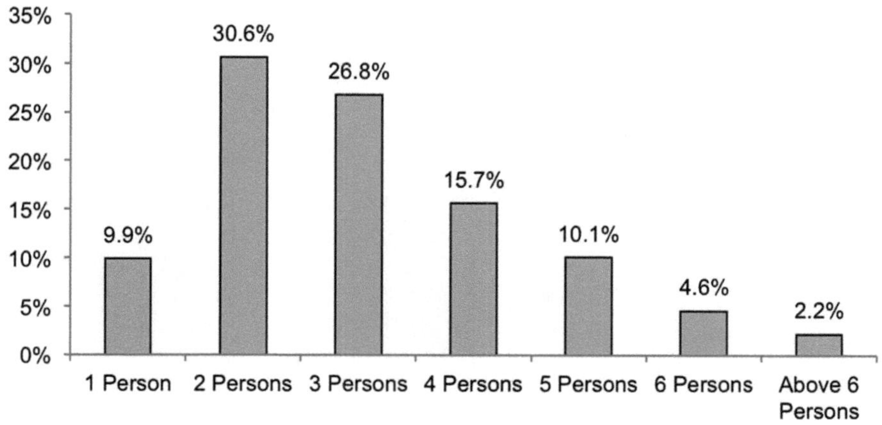

Chart 1.2 Ratios of different family sizes

Table 1.6 Age and gender structure

Item	Average age	Median value of age	Proportion of each age group (%)			
			Children	Labor force	The elderly	Total
Total	39	40	15.0	65.8	9.2	–
Male	38	39	16.1	65.8	18.1	–
Female	40	41	13.9	66.5	19.7	–
Gender ratio			123.5	102.3	94.6	103.7
Urban			122.5	98.7	94.6	100.2
Rural			125.0	108.4	95.5	109.5

Note Depending on the classification of ages in China, the children population refers to people under the age of 15; the labor force population refers to people over the age of 15 (including those who are 15 years old) and under the age of 60; and the elderly are those who are more than 60 years old. The gender ratio is the population's proportion of males and females among which the female population given that the base number is 100

Special Feature 1-1 Aggravating Gender Imbalance
From Chart 1.3, it is obvious that China still has a gender imbalance and the tendency may be even starker in both urban and rural areas with the imbalance being more obvious in the rural areas. By comparing the statistics, there are signs that the gender imbalance is growing more severe.

Special Feature 1-2 Gender Imbalance and Average Years of Schooling
The gender imbalance in not only manifested in terms of the difference in the proportion of males to females, but also the in difference in the average years of schooling males and females receive. As shown in Table 1.7, the average years of schooling that males receive significantly exceeds that of females. The biggest gap lies in the years of schooling between rural males and females, a difference of 1.7 years.

Chart 1.3 Gender ratio changing tendency

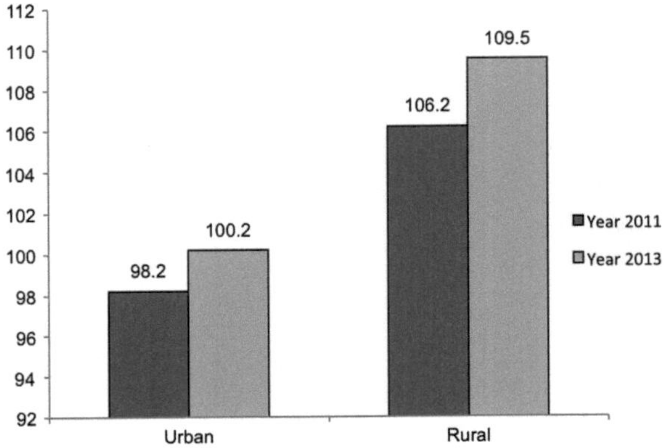

Table 1.7 Gender and average years of schooling

Region	Gender	Average years of schooling (Y)
Total	Male	9.9
	Female	8.7
Urban	Male	10.9
	Female	9.9
Rural	Male	8.2
	Female	6.5

Additionally, as shown in Table 1.8, among the labor force population, the average number of years of schooling for males also exceeds that of females. The largest gap lies in the years of schooling between rural males and females: 1.3 years.

Chart 1.4 also shows that the gender imbalance exists not only between urban and rural areas, but also reflects an imbalance based on geography and age distribution.

As each region's gender imbalance rises, the central region has seen the most rapid increase. In all of the groups, the gender imbalance among children is very significant. Overall, China's gender imbalance is intensifying.

Table 1.8 Gender and the average years of schooling among the labor force

Region	Gender	Average years of schooling (Y)
Total	Male	10.5
	Female	9.8
Urban	Male	11.5
	Female	11
Rural	Male	9
	Female	7.7

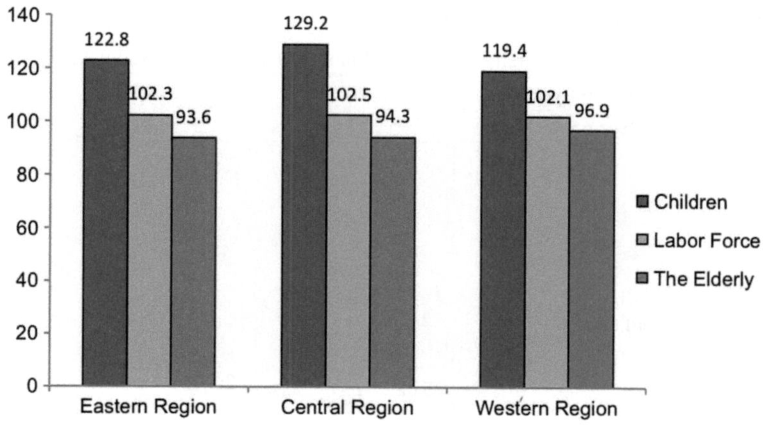

Chart 1.4 Gender ratio among different regions

1.3.3 Age Structure

As shown in Table 1.6, children, the labor force, and the elderly account for 15.0, 65.8, and 19.2 %of the total population, respectively. People who are more than 60 years old and 65 years old account for 19.2 and 11.5 % of the total population, respectively. As shown in Table 1.9, the total dependency ratio, the children's dependency ratio, and the elderly dependency ratio comprise 51.1, 22.1, and 29.0 % of the dependent population, respectively.

Special Feature 1-3 The Population is Aging

According to the 2013 CHFS statistics, two indicators can examine the condition of China's population aging. The first indicator is the proportion of people above the age of 60 to the entire population and the second indicator is the proportion of people above the age of 65 to the total population. Table 1.10 is the description of the standards and the actual status of aging population.

Table 1.9 Population burden analysis table

Region	Total dependency ratio (%)	Children's ratio (%)	The elderly ratio (%)
Total	51.1	22.1	29.0
East	50.9	21.3	30.6
Middle	50.3	22.3	28.0
West	52.1	24.6	27.5
Urban	48.9	20.4	28.5
Rural	54.7	25.0	29.7

Note The total dependency ratio refers to the proportion of children and the elderly to the labor force. The children's dependency ratio refers to the proportion of children to the labor force. The elderly dependency ratio refers to the proportion of the elderly to the labor force

Table 1.10 Status of the aging population

Indicator	Aging measurement	Standard (%)	Nationwide (%)
One	Over 60 years old	10	19.2
Two	Over 65 years old	7	11.3

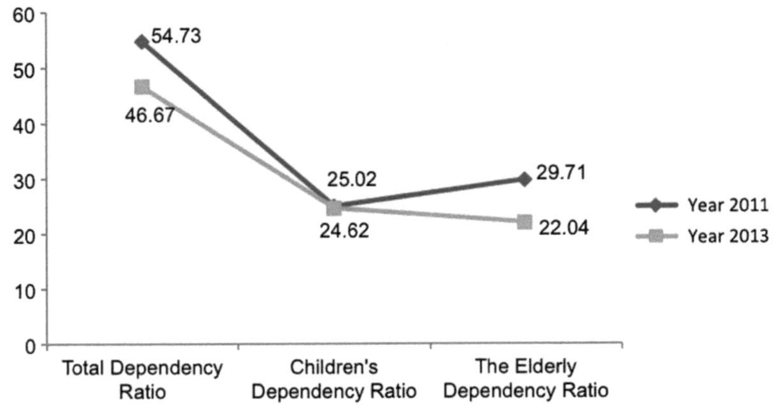

Chart 1.5 Dependency ratio comparison between year 2011 and 2013

As shown in Chart 1.5, both the vertical and horizontal indicators show China's aging population is increasing. Meanwhile, if the dependency ratio is taken into consideration, in 2013 the children's dependency ratio was below that of the elderly. The variation scope between the year 2013 and 2011 also reveals that when compared to the children's dependency ratio, the elderly dependency ratio has increased significantly and the aging population status will worsen regardless of population mobility. Chart 1.5 also indicates that the children's dependency ratio has fallen below the elderly dependency ratio in both the urban and rural areas. Hence, whether in urban or rural areas, the aging population has become a remarkable phenomenon and will continue to intensify.

1.3.4 Educational Background

As is shown in Table 1.11 and Chart 1.6, 8381 people are illiterate or semiliterate, accounting for 10.0 % of the survey sample. 16,952 people have primary school diplomas and account for 20.5 % of the survey sample. 25,725 people have junior high school diplomas, accounting for 31.1 % of the survey sample. 12,163 people have senior high school diplomas and account for 14.7 % of the survey sample. 4764 people have a technical secondary school or vocational school diploma, accounting for 5.8 % of the survey sample. 6307 people have a junior college or

Table 1.11 Overall educational background structure

Educational background	Number of people	Age (%)
Illiterate and semiliterate	8381	10.0
Primary school	16,952	20.5
Junior high school	25,725	31.1
Senior high school	12,163	14.7
Technical secondary school and vocational school	4764	5.8
Junior college and senior vocational school	6307	7.6
Bachelor's degree	7654	9.3
Master's degree	650	0.8
Doctoral degree	140	0.2

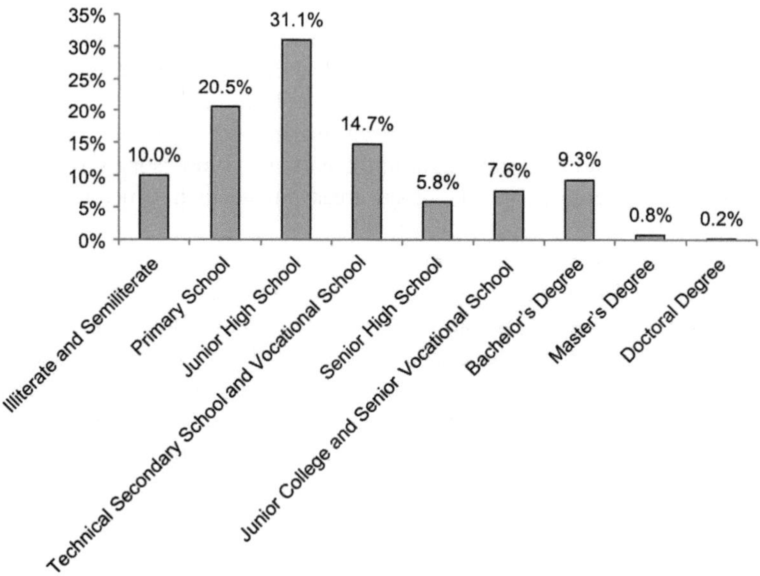

Chart 1.6 Overall educational background structure

senior vocational school diploma and account for 7.6 % of the survey sample. 7654 people have bachelor's degrees and account for 9.3 % of the survey sample. 790 people have a master's degree or higher, accounting for 1.0 % of the survey sample.

Table 1.11 shows that in 2013 China's proportion of illiterate or semiliterate people remained high and was virtually unchanged from the 2011 amount. The proportion of people with a junior high school education or lower fell slightly and the China's low educational attainment situation has not significantly improved. Its share in receiving higher education has increased remarkably, however, from 8.37 to 10.27 %. This reflects the impact of the enrollment expansion policy.

Table 1.12 Urban and rural education structure

Educational Background	Rural (%)	Urban (%)
Illiterate and semiliterate	16.6	6.2
Primary school	30.1	14.6
Junior high school	34.4	29.0
Senior high school	9.7	17.8
Technical secondary school and vocational school	3.0	7.4
Junior college and senior vocational school	2.7	10.6
Bachelor's degree	3.3	12.9
Master's degree	0.1	1.2
Doctoral degree	0.1	0.3

Meanwhile, there is an imbalance in the number of years of schooling between urban and rural areas and geographic regions. The more developed the region is, the more years of education the people have. Table 1.12 shows that obvious educational structural differences exist between urban and rural areas. Rural area households mainly end their education in the national compulsory stage, i.e. junior high school while more people in urban areas pursue their education for higher level.

Table 1.13 shows that, with regard to geographical distribution, the western region's level of education lags significantly behind those of the eastern and central regions. The proportion of people receiving higher education in the central and western is 8.31 and 8.61 %, respectively, far below 12.56 % in the eastern region.

Charts 1.7, 1.8 and 1.9 have revealed the distribution of education background of different age cohorts. Among people under the age of 35 (not included), people who have received more education accounted for 21.1 % of the age cohort. Among people between the ages of 35 and 50 (not included) or over the age of 50, however,

Table 1.13 Regional education structure

Educational background	Eastern (%)	Central (%)	Western (%)
Illiterate and semiliterate	8.16	10.00	13.18
Primary school	17.52	20.87	24.52
Junior high school	30.50	33.76	29.27
Senior high school	15.77	14.94	12.86
Technical secondary school and vocational school	6.67	5.30	4.89
Junior college and senior vocational school	8.82	6.52	6.97
Bachelor's degree	11.17	7.87	7.80
Master's degree	1.12	0.62	0.44
Doctoral degree	0.27	0.12	0.07

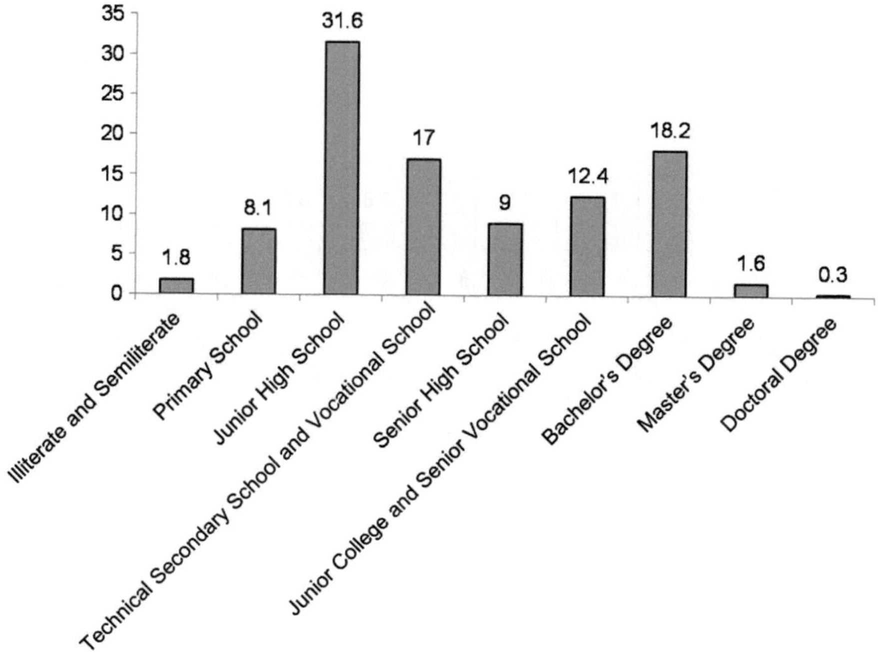

Chart 1.7 Educational background structure of interviewees below 35 years old (not including 35)

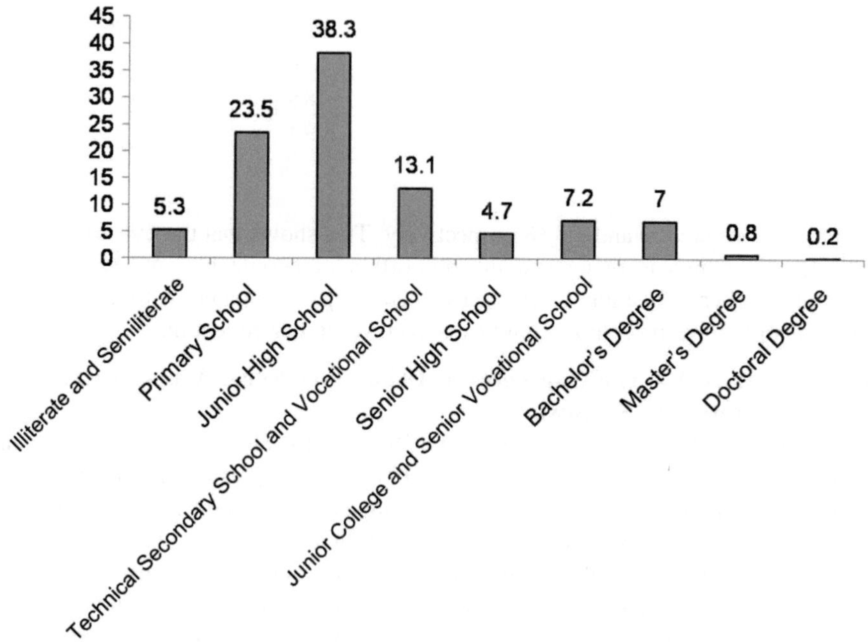

Chart 1.8 Educational background structure of interviewees between 35 and 50 years old (not including 50)

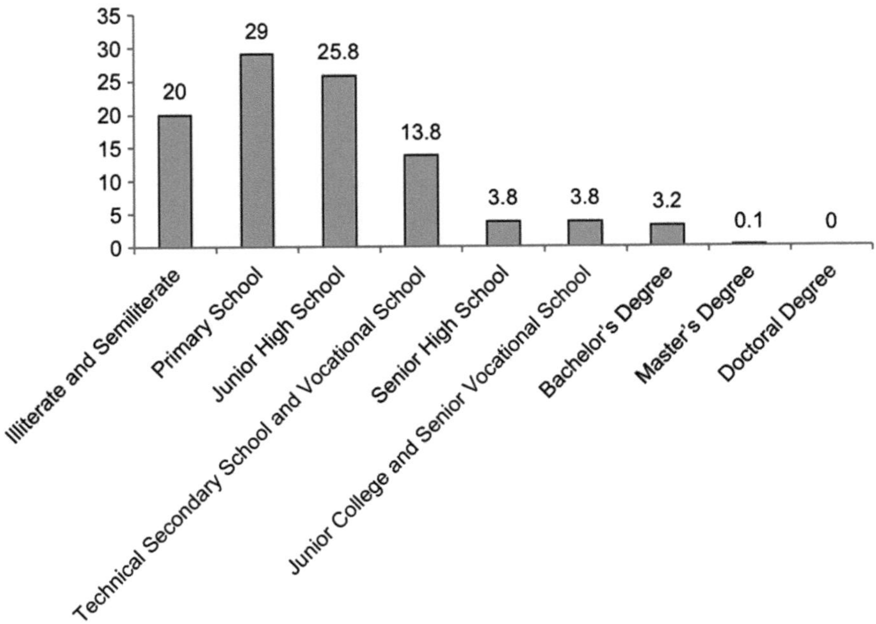

Chart 1.9 Educational background structure of interviewees above 50 years old

Table 1.14 Proportion of people born in the 1970s and 1980s with a bachelor's degree or higher

Category	People born in the 1970s (%)	People born in the 1980s (%)
Nationwide	10.6	21.6
Urban	15.5	28.9
Rural	1.2	9.1

the proportions are 8.0 and 3.3 %, respectively. This shows that the overall years of schooling in China is rising and the proportion of people in same age cohorts receiving higher education is gradually increasing. Compared with the elderly, young people have more opportunities to receive higher education.

Special Feature 1-4 The Gap between Urban and Rural Areas in Receiving Higher Education Is Narrowing

As shown in Table 1.14, people born in the 1970s and 1980s have become the main labor source. Among the people born in the 1970s, the proportion of urban residents who received higher education is nearly 13 times that of rural residents. Among people born in the 1980s, however, the proportion of urban residents receiving higher education is nearly three times that of rural residents. From these statistics, it is clear that although there is still great disparity in the higher education attainment level between urban and rural residents, great progress has been achieved as this disparity has been narrowed nearly ten times over the past ten years. At the same time, whether in urban or rural areas, the absolute proportion of those receiving a higher education has greatly increased. This also reflects the results of China promoting the development of higher education.

1.3.5 Marital Status

According to the sample conducted by CHFS in 2013, the number of unmarried people who were surveyed was 14,252, accounting for 17.2 % of the total number. The number of surveyed married people was 62,833, accounting for 76 % of the total number. The number of people who were cohabitating was 280, accounting for 0.3 % of the total number. The number of people who were separated and surveyed is 138, accounting for 0.2 % of the total number. The number of divorced people who were surveyed was 1118, accounting for 1.4 % of the total number. The number of widowed people who were surveyed was 4116, accounting for 5.0 % of the total number.

Feature 1-5 Differences in Marital Status Exist Between Urban and Rural Areas

According to the survey data conducted in 2013, there is a great disparity in the marital status between urban and rural areas. The proportion of married, cohabitating, separated, and divorced people in urban areas is higher than in rural areas. The proportion of unmarried people in the rural areas is higher than in the urban areas, as is shown in Table 1.15. Among the unmarried group (in this report, "the unmarried group" refers to unmarried men and women over the age of 30), there is a significant disparity in the amount of "leftover men" and "leftover women" in the urban and rural areas. As shown in Table 1.16, the proportion of "leftover men" in

Table 1.15 Proportion of marital status (*unit* %)

Region	Unmarried	Married	Cohabitated	Separated	Divorced	Widowed
Nationwide	17.2	75.9	0.3	0.2	1.4	5.0
Urban	16.6	76.4	0.4	0.2	1.7	4.7
Rural	18.3	75.1	0.2	0.2	0.8	5.4

Table 1.16 Distribution of unmarried status among people 30 Years old or older

Gender	Number	Urban		Rural	
		Proportion (%)	Years of schooling (Y)	Proportion (%)	Years of schooling (Y)
Male	533	43.2	10.3	73.6	7.6
Female	531	74.3	10.3	26.5	5.0
Total	1064	56.8	10.3	26.7	6.9

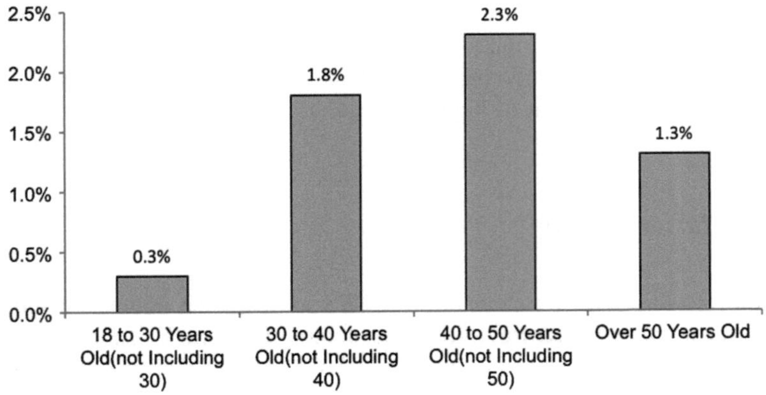

Chart 1.10 The divorce rate in different ages

Table 1.17 Unmarried group between the ages of 30 and 40

Gender	Years of schooling (Year)					
	Nationwide	Unmarried	Urban	Unmarried	Rural	Unmarried
Male	10.8	10.8	12.0	12.5	8.7	8.4
Female	10.2	12.2	11.5	13.2	7.6	9.2

the rural areas has surpassed that of the urban areas and the proportion of "leftover women" in urban areas has surpassed that of the rural areas. Compared with 2011, there is an obviously expanding disparity between the urban and rural areas. The underlying cause of the variation is the gender imbalance between urban and rural areas. As Table 1.10 shows, the gender ratio in the urban and rural areas is 100.2:100 and 109.5:100, respectively.

The urban divorce rate is nearly twice that of the rural areas, indicating that the marital status of urban residents may be more unstable than that of rural residents. At the same time, as shown in Chart 1.10, the most unstable age cohort in terms of marital status is 40–50 years old (not included), followed by 30–40 years old (not included).

In the urban areas, the number of widowed women is 3.5 times greater than the number of widowed men. This is consistent with the conclusion that, on average, women live longer than men.

Special Feature 1-6 "Leftover Men" and "Leftover Women"

The past few years have witnessed more and more dating TV shows in China. Also, on November 11, 2013, China's "Singles Day," Chinese electronics vendors yielded a record new-high sales volume of 35 billion RMB. These facts all reflect the care and love that society gives to its "leftovers." As is shown in Table 1.17, if unmarried people between the ages of 30 and 40 (not included) are examined, the proportion of "leftover men" to "leftover women" is 2.6:1, with a proportion of 2:1

in urban areas and 4.2:1 in rural areas. Statistics show that the problem of "leftover men" is more urgent. This is consistent with the population imbalance phenomenon.

Viewed from the perspective of the average years of schooling among unmarried females between the ages of 30 and 40 (not included), whether urban or rural, the average years of schooling for this age cohort is higher than that of the average level for all age cohorts. For this age cohort, the average years of schooling for urban females is higher than that of rural females. Among males between the ages of 30 and 40 (not included), the average number of years of schooling is lower than that of females. Whether in urban or rural areas, there is not a huge gap in the years of schooling between unmarried men and the national average.

Chapter 2
Rural Household Employment

CHFS (China Household Finance Survey) reports that the economically active rural population comprises 60.7 % of the overall rural population while the working population comprises 97.4 % of the economically active population. 50.6 % of the rural economically active population that is 60 or older still works. Among them, 91.0 % are engaged in agricultural activities. In terms of employment type, 56.6 % of the rural working population engages in agricultural work while 43.4 % is employed in non-agricultural work. Agricultural producers receive an average of 6.2 years of education with an average life expectancy of 50.7 years. Males account for only 49.5 % of the rural population. Agricultural producing, non-agricultural labor, and agricultural and non-agricultural hybrid households (hereafter referred to as "hybrids") account for 37.6, 31.8, and 30.6 % of household employment sources, respectively. In terms of both individual employment and household employment, there's a clear tendency towards non-agricultural employment.

2.1 Working Population

According to the People's Republic of China statistical system, the economically active population refers to people who are at least 16 years old and work in economic production or service activities over a certain period of time. These people, also referred to as the labor force, participate or are expected to participate in social economic activities. Together, the employed population and the unemployed population comprise the economically active population.

According to CHFS, the rural economically active population refers to the portion of the rural population that is at least 16 years old and is employed, unemployed, or seasonally employed. Table 2.1 illustrates the statistics of the rural economically active population.

As is illustrated in Table 2.1, the rural economically active population accounts for 60.7 % of the rural population, higher than the 54.2 % nationwide. The rural

L. Gan et al., *Report on the Development of Household Finance in Rural China (2014)*, DOI 10.1007/978-981-10-0409-4_2

Table 2.1 Rural economically active population and employment (*unit* %)

	Rural	Eastern region	Central region	Western region	National
Economically active population/total population	60.7	59.4	62.3	60.2	54.2
Working population/economically active population	97.4	96.8	97.8	97.5	94.6

working population accounts for 97.4 % of the rural economically active population, slightly higher than the national statistic of 94.6 %.

In terms of geographic distribution, the eastern region's rural economically active population rate is 59.4 %, slightly lower than the national statistic of 60.7 %. The western region's corresponding figure has a generally similar overall figure. The ratio of the central region's rural economically active population is higher than the national statistic of 60.7 %. The working population accounts for 96.8, 97.8, and 97.5 % of the rural economically active populations in the eastern, western, and central regions, respectively, with only slight differences between them.

Since the proportion of the rural economically active population and the working population are significantly higher than the average national figure, this report will further analyze age structure of these two groups. Table 2.2 demonstrates the proportion of the rural economically active population and working population that is at least 60 years old.

As is shown in Table 2.2, the rural economically active population accounts for 50.6 % of the rural population, much higher than 13.5 % for urban areas. Meanwhile, the rural working population accounts for 50.0 % of the rural population, which is also much higher than the 12.2 % in urban areas. Thus, the difference between the rural economically active population ratio and the working population ratio stems from the employment of rural seniors.

CHFS classified China's working population's employment types into seven groups: employed by others; self-employed; agricultural activities; people who retire and are subsequently rehired by the same organization (hereafter referred to as "rehired"); freelancing; seasonally employed; and others. Agricultural activities are the only type of agricultural activity while the remaining employment types are non-agricultural activities. Table 2.3 shows the employment categories of the rural working population that is at least 60 years old.

Table 2.3 allows for the inference that of the majority of the rural working population that is at least 60 years old, 91.0 %, is engaged in agricultural activities.

Table 2.2 Rural economically active population and working population (*unit* Yuan)

	Rural	Urban	Nationwide
Economically active population	50.6	13.5	31.6
Working population	50.0	12.2	30.6

Table 2.3 Employment categories of rural working population aged 60 and over (*unit %*)

	Rural
Agricultural activities	91.0
Non-agricultural activities	9.0

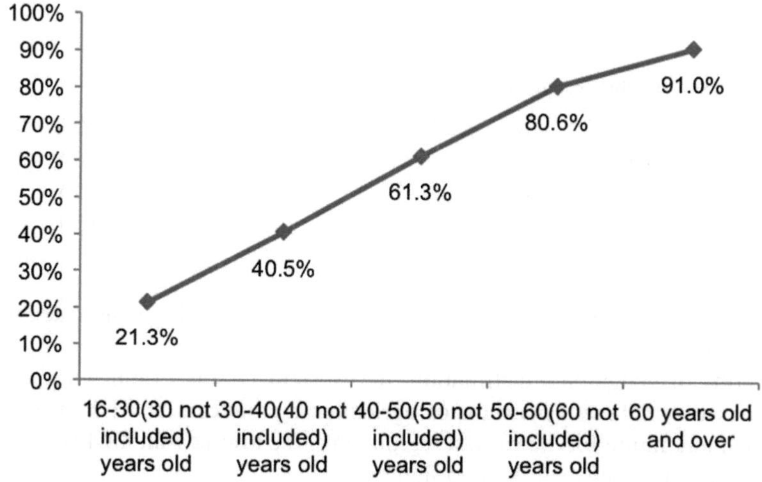

Chart 2.1 Proportions of rural population of different ages engaged in agricultural activities

Chart 2.1 displays the proportion of agricultural producers in the rural working population in terms of age distribution by separating the age cohorts by ten-year intervals. As is shown in Chart 2.1, the proportion rises along with age. 21.3 % of the population is between the ages of 16–30 while 91.0 % of the rural working population that is at least 60 years old engages in agricultural activities. The aforementioned statistics support the conclusion that there are less rural young people engaging in agricultural activities than rural seniors. In addition, rural seniors who have reached the age of 60 still participate in farming regardless of having reached retirement age.

2.2 Employment Categories

Table 2.4 illustrates the rural working population's employment categories. 30.7 % of the national working population is engaged in agricultural activities while 69.3 % is engaged in non-agricultural activities. This indicates that the national population's major employers are secondary and tertiary industries. 56.6 % of the rural working population is agricultural producing while non-agricultural workers account for 43.4 % of the rural working population. There is an obvious tendency

Table 2.4 Employment categories (*unit* %)

	Rural	Eastern region	Central region	Western region	National
Agricultural activities	56.6	48.4	58.7	61.5	30.7
Nonagricultural activities	43.4	51.6	41.3	38.5	69.3

Table 2.5 Demographic features of the rural working population (*unit* Yuan)

	Years of education (years)	Age (years)	Male ratio (%)
Rural working population	7.4	43.9	56.6
Agricultural producers	6.2	50.7	49.5
Non-agricultural workers	9.0	35.6	65.4

towards non-agricultural employment based on the employment categories of China's rural working population.

In terms of geographic distribution, the western region's rural working population has the highest proportion of agricultural producers at 61.5 % while the corresponding figure for the eastern region ranks the lowest with 48.4 %. There is a 13.1 % difference between the two figures.

Table 2.5 shows the rural working population's demographic features, including years of education, age, and ratio of males residing in the rural areas. The rural population engaged in agricultural activities has an average of 6.2 years of education while the corresponding figure for the rural population engaged in non-agricultural activities is 9.0 years. This indicates that agricultural producers received 2.8 years less education than non-agricultural workers. The average age of agricultural producers is 50.7 years while the corresponding figure for non-agricultural workers is 35.6 years. The 15.1 year discrepancy indicates that agricultural producers are older. Meanwhile, 49.5 % of agricultural producers are male while the figure for male non-agricultural workers is 65.4 %, higher than the former. The general profile of agricultural producers is that they are less educated, elderly, and less are males.

2.3 Employment Type

Table 2.6 describes employment types of the rural working population's non-agricultural workers. 71.3 % of non-agricultural workers are employed by others or institutions, 15.9 % are self-employed, and 9.6 % are freelancers. These three types comprise 96.7 % of non-agricultural workers.

In terms of geographic distribution, the three aforementioned employment categories account for 97.2, 96.5, and 96.4 % in the eastern, central, and western

Table 2.6 Types of non-agricultural activities that the rural working population engages (*unit* %)

	Rural	Eastern region	Central region	Western region
Employed by others	71.3	69.8	71.4	72.8
Self-employed	15.9	18.0	16.2	13.1
Freelance jobs	9.6	9.4	8.9	10.5
Seasonal jobs	2.4	1.7	2.7	2.9
Rehired workers	0.1	0.1	0.1	0.1
Others	0.7	1.0	0.7	0.6
Total	100.0	100.0	100.0	100.0

regions, respectively. There is little difference regarding this type of employment. Obvious differences can be seen in self-employment, however, which accounts for 18.0, 16.2, and 13.1 % of non-agricultural workers in the eastern, central, and western regions, respectively. There is a 4.9 % discrepancy between the highest 18.0 % in the eastern region and the lowest 13.1 % in the western region.

2.4 Employment Distribution

Table 2.7 shows the distribution of employment categories and two other types of employment. In terms of occupations, technicians, business and financial operation occupations, service industry workers, industrial occupations and transport occupations, and other occupations account for 34.6, 23.9, and 14.1 % of the national working population, respectively. The rural working population shares a similar

Table 2.7 Employment distribution of non-agricultural workers in the rural working population (*unit* Yuan)

Occupations	Rural	Nationwide
Technicians	32.1	34.6
Civil servants	8.6	15.2
Business and catering employees	18.3	23.9
Agriculture, forestry, animal husbandry, fishing and hydraulic engineering employees[a]	6.7	1.9
Manufacturing, construction and transportation employees	28.4	14.1
Management occupations	5.7	10.1
Military occupations	0.2	0.2
Total	100.0	100.0

[a]Here, agriculture, forestry, animal husbandry, fishing, and hydraulic engineering employees refer to people who work for corresponding agricultural businesses (e.g. agricultural enterprises). Since the businesses are not family-owned, people working for those businesses are classified as non-agricultural employees

employment distribution pattern. The ratio of the three employment types is 32.1, 18.3, and 28.4 %, respectively, totaling 79.5 %. One noteworthy difference is that the ratio of rural population engaged in industrial and transport occupations is relatively higher with a 14.3 % discrepancy.

2.5 Employment Industries

Table 2.8 shows the rural population's employment industries. As is illustrated in Table 2.8, the main industries of employment nationwide are manufacturing, construction and transportation, warehousing, and postal services which account for 16.0, 10.9, and 8.2 %, respectively, totaling 35.1 %. Compared with national statistics, the rural working population mainly engages in manufacturing, construction and agriculture, forestry, fishing, and hunting. Manufacturing and construction in particular account for 22.0 and 25.4 %, respectively, for a total of 47.4 %.

Table 2.8 Industry of employment of rural non-agricultural employees (*unit* %)

Industry	Rural	Nationwide
Agriculture, forestry, fishing and hunting	9.3	4.0
Mining	4.4	1.9
Manufacturing	22.0	16.0
Electric power, coal gas, water manufacturing and supply	3.2	3.7
Construction	25.4	10.9
Transportation, warehousing and postal services	5.0	8.2
Information, computer service and software	0.7	3.2
Wholesale and retail	3.7	7.0
Hospitality and catering	4.3	4.6
Financial services	0.7	4.3
Real estate	0.9	1.6
Leasing and business services	1.6	3.6
Scientific research, technical services and geological exploration	0.1	0.7
Water conservancy, environmental industry and management of public facilities	0.8	1.4
Resident services and other service industries	7.0	8.0
Education	4.6	8.1
Health care, social security and welfare	3.7	6.3
Cultural industry, sport industry and entertainment industry	0.5	1.9
Public administration and social organizations	2.1	4.6
Total	100.0	100.0

2.6 Categories of Household Occupations

This report has grouped rural households into three categories based on the household members' occupations: agricultural producers, non-agricultural employees, and hybrids. Among rural working households, being an agricultural producer indicates farming as the only occupation for all household members while households with no work related to agricultural activities fall into the non-agricultural employee category. The rest belong to the hybrid category whose household members are occupied with farming as well as non-agricultural activities.

Agricultural producers, non-agricultural labor, and hybrid occupations account for 37.6, 31.8, and 30.6 % of rural working households, respectively, as shown in Table 2.9. The statistics demonstrate the continuously changing occupation pattern of China's rural working households. Comparing the hybrid households with both occupation and non-agricultural employees (which constitute the majority of rural working households), agricultural producers only comprise slightly more than one third of households. This reflects the trend of rural Chinese households participating in more non-agricultural activities.

With respect to regional differences, non-agricultural employees make up 40.4 % of working households in the eastern region; hybrid households comprise 39.4 % of those in the central region. There are more agricultural producers and hybrid households in the western region than non-agricultural employees which account for approximately 25.4 % of working households. These figures correspond with the economic development disparity between Eastern China and Western China.

Table 2.10 shows the age cohorts of rural households with different types of employment. The average ages of agricultural producers, non-agricultural employees, and hybrid employees are 40.2, 37.6, and 36.2 years, respectively. It

Table 2.9 Employment types of rural working households (*unit* %)

Household employment type	Rural	Eastern region	Central region	Western region
Agricultural producers	37.6	25.1	33.6	36.2
Non-agricultural employees	31.8	40.4	27.0	25.4
A mix of agricultural and nonagricultural employees	30.6	34.5	39.4	38.4

Table 2.10 Age levels of rural households of different employment types (*unit* year (age))

Employment type	Rural	Eastern region	Central region	Western region
Agricultural producers	40.2	41.9	40.1	39.2
Nonagricultural employees	37.6	38.1	37.1	37.5
Hybrid employees (a mix of agricultural and non-agricultural employment)	36.2	37.3	34.9	36.7

Table 2.11 Average years of education received by rural working households of different employment types (*unit* year)

Employment type	Rural	Eastern region	Central region	Western region
Agricultural producers	6.7	6.9	7.1	6.2
Nonagricultural employees	8.1	8.6	7.8	7.7
Hybrid households	7.8	7.9	8.0	7.5

Table 2.12 Average income of rural households of different employment types (*unit* Yuan/year)

Employment type	Rural	Eastern region	Central region	Western region
Agricultural producers	20,219	19,024	22,242	19,092
Non-agricultural employees	55,048	63,727	46,653	51,386
Hybrid households (a mix of agricultural and non-agricultural employees)	42,591	38,546	46,395	41,855

can be inferred that the average agricultural producer's age is higher than that of hybrid employees. In terms of regional distribution, agricultural producers in the western region are younger than agricultural producers in the eastern and central regions with an average of 39.2 years. For non-agricultural workers and hybrid employees, their average age in the central region is lower than those in the eastern and western regions.

Table 2.11 demonstrates the average years of education received by rural households with different types of employment. The average years of education for agricultural producers, non-agricultural workers, and hybrid employees were 6.7, 8.1, and 7.8 years, respectively. This leads to the conclusion that non-agricultural workers received more years of education. To analyze these figures from a regional perspective, this report concludes that non-agricultural workers receive the highest level education followed by hybrid households. Agricultural producers receive the least education.

Table 2.12 illustrates the average income of households with different types of employment. The average incomes of agricultural producers, non-agricultural workers and hybrid workers are 20,219 RMB, 55,048 RMB, and 42,591 RMB, respectively. The household income of non-agricultural workers is 2.7 times greater than that of agricultural producers while the household income of rural hybrid households is 2.1 times higher than that of agricultural producers. The household incomes of both non-agricultural and hybrid workers are much higher than that of agricultural producers. This conclusion can also be drawn from analyzing the figures from a regional perspective. The household incomes of rural agricultural producers and rural hybrid workers in the central region are relatively high while non-agricultural workers in the eastern region enjoy high incomes.

Chapter 3
Rural Household Incomes

This chapter analyzes rural household incomes. Studies have shown that overall rural household income is relatively low and is only equal to 58.8 % of the national average income. This shows the huge household income gap between rural and urban households in China. In terms of regional differences, rural household incomes in China's eastern region rank the highest with 41,786 Yuan per household followed by rural households in the central region with 35,046 Yuan per household. Rural households in the western region rank the lowest with 33,183 Yuan per household. In terms of income sources, 48.6 % of rural household income is employment income, 21.7 % is agricultural income, and 17.8 % is transfer income. Employment income's proportion of total income is highest for rural households in the eastern region at 50.5 % followed by the central region with 48.5 % and the western region ranking the lowest of the three regions at 46.3 %. This indicates that non-agricultural income has become a crucial part of rural household income. Eastern rural households have higher business incomes than the other two regions which is consistent with the region's high self-employment ratio. The transfer incomes of rural households in the eastern, central, and western regions are 8923 Yuan, 4675 Yuan, and 6135 Yuan, respectively. Eastern rural households have higher transfer incomes than the other two regions. The eastern region also has higher household income disparity than the central and western regions.

3.1 Income Overview

3.1.1 Overall Income of Rural Households

Rural household income includes agricultural and non-agricultural income. Agricultural income refers to the net income of agricultural activities which equals total agricultural income minus cost. Non-agricultural income includes employment income, business income, property income, and transfer income.

L. Gan et al., *Report on the Development of Household Finance in Rural China (2014)*, DOI 10.1007/978-981-10-0409-4_3

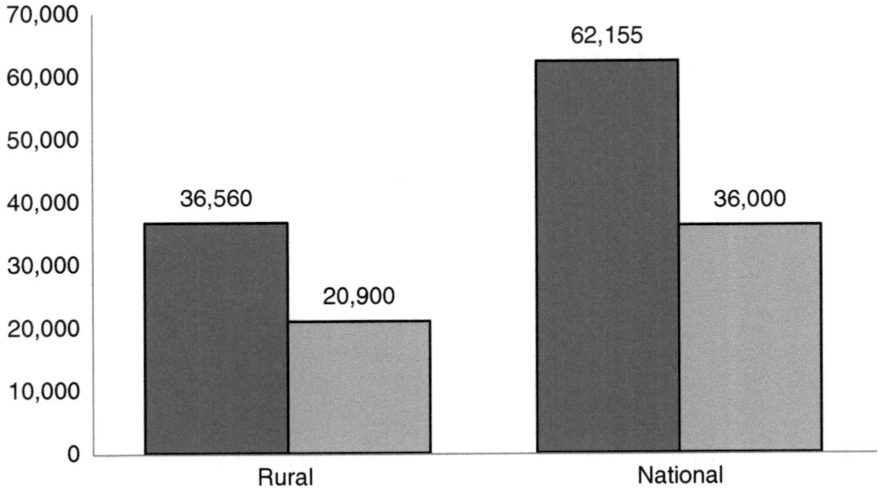

Chart 3.1 Rural household income

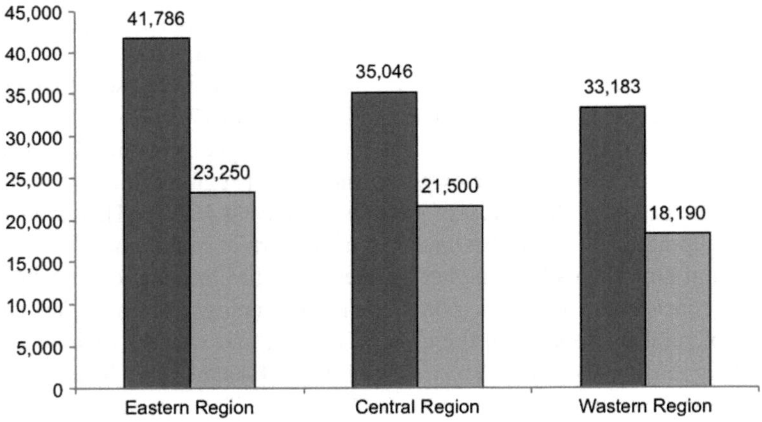

Chart 3.2 Rural households income in Eastern, Central, Western Region

As is shown in Chart 3.1, the gross income of Chinese households is 62,155 Yuan per household and the median is 36,000 Yuan. In comparison, the rural household income is far below the national figure. Rural household income is 36,560 Yuan per household (equal to only 58.8 % that of national figure) while the median is 20,900 Yuan (equal to only 58.1 % of national figure). This indicates that there is a huge household income disparity between urban and rural households in China.

From a regional perspective, China's rural household income decreases from the eastern region to the western region. The average total rural household income in the eastern, central, and western regions is 41,786 Yuan, 35,046 Yuan, and 33,183 Yuan, respectively. The median is 23,250 Yuan, 21,500 Yuan, and 18,190 Yuan, respectively. The rural household income in the eastern region is 1.3 times that of the western region (Chart 3.2).

3.1.2 Income Sources of Rural Households

Table 3.1 shows the income sources of rural households. Rural Chinese household income includes agricultural income, employment income, business income, property income, and transfer income with an average of 7927 Yuan, 17,764 Yuan, 3820 Yuan, 529 Yuan, and 6520 Yuan which account for 21.7, 48.6, 10.4, 1.4, and 17.8 %, respectively. This leads to the conclusion that employment income contributes the most to rural household income and accounts for nearly half of total income, followed by agricultural income and transfer income.

Rural household income differs not only in quantity but also in sources by region. The agricultural income, employment income, business income, property income and transfer income of rural eastern households are 5303 Yuan, 21,122 Yuan, 5728 Yuan, 709 Yuan, and 8923 Yuan, respectively. The main sources of income are employment income, transfer income, and business income which account for 50.5, 21.4, and 13.7 % of total household income, respectively. At 12.7 %, the proportion of agricultural income in rural eastern households is much lower than that inthe central and western regions while the proportion of business income is relatively higher.

The agricultural income, employment income, business income, property income and transfer income of central rural households are 10,596 Yuan, 17,013 Yuan, 2461 Yuan, 300 Yuan, and 4675 Yuan, respectively. The main sources of income are employment income, agricultural income, and transfer income, accounting for 48.5, 30.2, and 13.3 % of total household income, respectively. In contrast, agricultural income accounts for nearly one-third of total household income in central rural households and is higher than in the eastern region.

The agricultural income, employment income, business income, property income and transfer income of western rural households is 7682 Yuan, 15,366

Table 3.1 Income sources of rural households

Income resource	Average income (Yuan)	Proportion (%)
Agricultural income	7927	21.7
Employment income	17,764	48.6
Business income	3820	10.4
Property income	529	1.5
Transfer income	6520	17.8
Total income	36,560	100.0

Table 3.2 Sources of income in rural households in the Eastern, Central, and Western Regions

	Eastern region		Central region		Western region	
	Average income (Yuan)	Proportion (%)	Average income (Yuan)	Proportion (%)	Average income (Yuan)	Proportion (%)
Agricultural income	5303	12.7	10,596	30.2	7682	23.1
Employment income	21,122	50.5	17,013	48.5	15,366	46.3
Business income	5728	13.7	2461	7.0	3408	10.3
Property income	709	1.7	300	1.0	593	1.8
Transfer income	8923	21.4	4675	13.3	6135	18.5
Total income	41,786	100.0	35,046	100.0	33,183	100.0

Note The fact that the average agricultural income in rural households in the eastern region is lower than in the central region results from the proportion of agricultural producers being lower than in the central region. The proportions of agricultural producers in the eastern, central, and western regions are 59.6, 73.0, and 74.6 %, respectively. Meanwhile, the loss rate of agricultural producers in the eastern, central, and western regions is 7.8, 4.6, and 5.6 %, respectively

Yuan, 3408 Yuan, 593 Yuan, and 6135 Yuan, respectively. The main income sources are employment income, agricultural income, and transfer income which account for 46.3, 23.1, and 18.5 % of total income, respectively. This is similar to the eastern region (Table 3.2).

3.2 Agricultural Income

Agricultural income refers to the net income from agricultural production and operation activities. It is calculated as gross agricultural income minus agricultural production cost. Meanwhile, it also includes food and monetary subsidies that households obtain from agricultural production and operation activities. Agricultural production costs are made up of employment costs and other costs from related activities.

Table 3.3 describes rural households' income from agricultural production and operation, including gross income, production costs, and agricultural net income. As shown in the table, rural households in China earn a gross income of 17,517 Yuan from agricultural production and operation activities, with production costs of 9590 Yuan, 54.7 % cost rate, and a mean agricultural net income of 7927 Yuan.

In accordance with the data, agricultural income varies significantly among different regions. Rural households in the eastern region obtain agricultural gross incomes of 16,909 Yuan and spend 11,606 Yuan on production cost. This means that the cost rate is as high as 68.6 % and the agricultural net income reaches 5303

Table 3.3 Agricultural income of rural households (*unit* Yuan)

Sample range	Gross agricultural income	Agricultural production cost	Cost rate (%)	Agricultural net income (mean)
Rural	17,517	9590	54.7	7927
Eastern	16,909	11,606	68.6	5303
Central	20,359	9763	48.0	10,596
Western	15,198	7516	49.5	7682

Table 3.4 Agricultural subsidies of rural households

Sample range	Percentage of households with subsidies	Agricultural subsidies (mean, Yuan)
Rural	53.6	389
Eastern	41.6	205
Central	67.2	648
Western	51.1	298

Yuan. Gross income for rural households in the central region is 20,359 Yuan and they have production costs 9763 Yuan, cost rates of 48 %, and agricultural net income of up to 10,596 Yuan. Rural households in the western region obtain agricultural gross income of 15,198 Yuan with production costs of 7516 Yuan, cost rates of 49.5 %, and agricultural net income of 7682 Yuan. In summary, the cost of agricultural production is the highest in the eastern region.

Table 3.4 illustrates the condition of agricultural subsidies that rural households receive from participating in agricultural production and operation activities. In general, 53.6 % of rural households acquire subsidies at an average of 389 Yuan. Rural households in the central region prevail both in the number of households with subsidies, accounting for 67.2 %, and in the amount of money they receive, an average of 648 Yuan per household. In comparison, eastern rural households not only earn less agricultural income, but also obtain the least amount with only 41.6 % of households receiving subsidies at an average of 205 Yuan. Rural households in the west rank in the middle, accounting for 51.1 % and an average amount of 298 Yuan.

3.3 Non-agricultural Income

3.3.1 Income from Wages and Salaries

Income from wages and salaries is the most significant source of gross income from rural households. It comprises 48.6 % of gross income and is mainly comprised of after-tax money wages, bonuses, and subsidies as well as income from primary and

Table 3.5 Income from wages and salaries of rural households

Sample range	Mean	Median
Rural	17,764	0
Total	30,119	9000

Table 3.6 Income from wages and salaries of rural households in different areas

Sample range	Mean (Yuan)	Percentage of households with income from wages and salaries (%)
Eastern	21,122	48.2
Central	17,013	44.3
Western	15,366	42.7

secondary jobs. As shown in Table 3.5, the average income from wages and salaries in rural households is 17,764 Yuan, far below the total level. The total average level is 30,119 Yuan and is 1.7 times that of rural households. The median wages and salaries income of rural households is 0 Yuan, illustrating that at least half of rural households have little income from this source.

Table 3.6 gives a summary of the regional disparities in rural households' wages and salaried incomes. The average numbers in the eastern, central, and western regions are 21,122 Yuan, 17,013 Yuan, and 15,366 Yuan, respectively, with rural households in the east ranking highest and the west ranking lowest. The proportion of households with income from wages and salaries also decreases from the east to the west, accounting for 48.2, 44.3, and 42.7 %, respectively.

3.3.2 *Business Income*

Business income refers to the net income households obtain from industrial and business operation activities, including individual businesses and self-employed businesses. Only 9.1 % of rural households engage in industrial and business operation, far below the total average of 14.2 %. In addition to a weaker desire to participate, rural households also obtain less net income from business operations. Table 3.7 shows that the mean value of business income of rural households in China is 3820 Yuan and only accounts for 38.8 % of the total amount.

Table 3.7 Business income of rural households

Sample range	Mean (Yuan)	Median (Yuan)
Rural	3820	0
Overall	9849	0

Comparing the different regions, the proportion of households engaging in industrial and business operations in the east is the highest in the country at 10.8 % and is 2.2 and 2.4 % higher than the central and western regions, respectively. As for the net income of operation, the mean value in the eastern, central, and western areas are 5728 Yuan, 2461 Yuan, and 3408 Yuan with the east ranking the highest (Table 3.8).

Table 3.9 demonstrates the distribution of rural households' industrial and business activities. It can be seen that the distribution concentrates on several industries, including the wholesale and retail industry, transportation, communications, storage and postal industries, manufacturing, and accommodation and catering, accounting for 46.1, 15.9, 10.0, and 9.6 %, separately (and respectively) and a joint total of 81.6 %.

Table 3.10 shows the business condition of rural households participating in industrial and business operations. Among those households, 79.6 % earn a profit, 5.4 % suffer a loss, and 15.0 % break even. Compared with all households engaged in industrial and business operations, the percentage of profiting rural households is 2.3 % higher. Besides, the eastern region has the largest proportion of profitable households.

Table 3.8 Business income of rural households in different areas

Sample range	Mean (Yuan)	Percentage of households with business income (%)
Eastern	5728	10.8
Central	2461	8.6
Western	3408	8.4

Table 3.9 Distribution of rural households industrial and business activities (*unit* %)

Industries	Rural	Total
Wholesale and retail	46.1	43.0
Transport, communications, storage and postal	15.9	11.9
Manufacturing	10.0	7.5
Accommodation and catering	9.6	11.4
Resident service and other service industries	5.0	6.3
Construction	4.1	5.9
Leasing and business services	2.8	4.4
Health, social security and welfare	2.3	1.4
Culture, sports and entertainment	1.2	2.2
Production and supply of electricity, gas and water	1.0	0.8
Information, computer and software	0.5	2.3
Other	1.5	2.9

Table 3.10 Business condition of rural households in industrial and business operations (*unit* %)

Operating status	Rural	Eastern	Central	Western	Overall
Profit	79.6	81.0	79.4	78.0	77.3
Loss	5.4	3.8	6.8	5.9	6.4
Even	15.0	15.2	13.8	16.1	16.3
Total	100.0	100.0	100.0	100.0	100.0

Table 3.11 Income from investments of rural households

Types of income	Rural		Total	
	Mean (Value)	Percentage (%)	Mean (Value)	Percentage (%)
Financial investments	113	21.4	794	37.2
Renting houses and lands	416	78.6	1339	62.8
Income from properties	529	100.0	2133	100.0

3.3.3 Income from Properties

Income from properties mainly consists of income from financial investments and rent houses and land. Income from financial investments includes income from interest on time deposits, stock price differences and dividends, bond investments, fund price difference and dividend, derivatives investments, wealth management products, non-RMB asset investments, and gold investments. Income from rent houses and land includes the rent from land and dividends on land shares as well as the rent from houses and stores.

In rural China, 16.4 % of households possess income from properties, 7.1 % lower than the total level. Table 3.11 shows the income from properties of rural households in China and its structure. The mean value of investment incomes for rural households is 529 Yuan, much lower than the nationwide average of 2133 Yuan and only reaches 24.8 % of the total level. From the perspective of its structure, rent from land and houses comprise the majority, accounting for 78.6 %. Statistics show that rural households have much lower incomes from properties than all households, especially income from financial investments and rent houses and lands. Their incomes are 7.0 and 3.4 times lower, respectively.

The percentages of households with income from properties in eastern, central, and western China are 21.1, 13.9, and 14.7 %, respectively. It is obvious that the east has the highest percentage and is 7.2 and 6.4 % higher than the central and western areas. Table 3.12 illustrates the regional disparities of rural households regarding income from properties Income from rural households' investments is 709 Yuan in the east, 300 Yuan in the central region, and 593 Yuan in the west with the eastern region having the highest level.

Table 3.12 Regional disparities of income from investments of rural households

Types of income	Eastern		Central		Western	
	Mean (value)	Percentage (%)	Mean (value)	Percentage (%)	Mean (value)	Percentage (%)
Financial investments	216	30.4	50	16.8	80	13.5
Renting houses and lands	493	69.6	250	83.2	512	86.5
Income from properties	709	100.0	300	100.0	593	100.0

Analyzing income from properties, income from financial investments comprises the largest proportion at 30.4 %. The mean value is 216 Yuan and is 4.3 times that of rural households in the central region and 2.7 times that of the western region. This means that rural households in the east have stronger financial and investment awareness. As for income from rent houses and lands, the mean value in the eastern regions is 493 Yuan, comprising 69.6 % of total income from properties; in the central region it is 250 Yuan, comprising 83.2 %; and 512 Yuan, 86.5 %, in the western region.

3.3.4 *Transfer Income*

Transfer income consists of income from relationships, housing and land subsidies, agricultural subsidies, retirement and pension income, insurance income, and income from other sources. Income from relationships includes income received on holidays such as the Spring Festival, Mid-Autumn Festival, weddings and funerals, income for education, medical services and living expenses, inheritances, and other income. As for housing and land subsidies, the majority is comprised of monetary subsidies and reimbursement (based on temporal value) for housing demolition as well as monetary compensation for land expropriation. Agricultural subsidies are composed of monetary and in-kind subsidies.

As shown in Table 3.13, although 80.4 % of rural households enjoy transfer income, their income level is still far below the national level. The average is 15,457 Yuan with a median of 2300 Yuan. Transfer income in rural households,

Table 3.13 Income from transfer in rural households

	Rural	Total
Household percentage (%)	80.4	81.4
Mean (Yuan)	6520	15,457
Median (Yuan)	1456	2300

however, reaches less than half the total level, with the average being 6520 Yuan and the median being 1456 Yuan.

In terms of transfer income structure, income from relationships, compensation from land expropriation and housing demolition, retirement and pension income, and transfer income from other sources of rural households are 1480 Yuan, 1287 Yuan, 2018 Yuan, 1113 Yuan, and 622 Yuan, respectively, accounting for 22.7, 19.7, 30.9, 17.1, and 9.5 % of total transfer income, respectively. This shows that the majority of rural households' transfer income comes from retirement and pension income, income from relationships, and income from land expropriation and housing demolition compensation. Of the total, they comprise 73.3 %. Compared with the overall condition, income from relationships and compensation for land expropriation and housing demolition comprise a larger proportion in rural areas, and they are 8.9 and 8.3 % higher than the total level, respectively. Rural retirement and pension income, however, is 21.3 % lower than the total and accounts for a smaller proportion. This shows that rural social security systems still have room for improvement (Table 3.14).

Table 3.15 demonstrates the disparity of transfer income of rural households in different regions. As shown in the table, the highest percentage of rural households with transfer income is in the western region, accounting for 83.0 %. This is followed by 80.3 % in the central region and 77.9 % in the eastern region. The mean transfer incomes in the eastern, central, and western areas are 8923 Yuan, 4675 Yuan, and 6135 Yuan, respectively. Since the mean value in the eastern region is nearly twice as much as the central region, regional disparities in transfer

Table 3.14 Composition of income from investments of rural households

Types of income	Rural		Total	
	Mean (value)	Percentage (%)	Mean (value)	Percentage (%)
Income from relationships	1480	22.7	2128	13.8
Compensation of land expropriation and housing demolition	1287	19.7	1766	11.4
Retirement and pension income	2018	30.9	8.071	52.2
Insurance income	1113	17.1	2417	15.6
Other sources	622	9.6	1075	7.0
Income from transfer	6520	100.0	15,457	100.0

Table 3.15 Regional disparities of transfer income of rural households

	Eastern	Central	Western
Percentage of households with transfer income (%)	77.9	80.3	83.0
Mean (Yuan)	8923	4675	6135
Median (Yuan)	1400	1400	1520

Table 3.16 Composition of transfer income of rural households in different regions

Types of income	Eastern		Central		Western	
	Mean (value)	Percentage (%)	Mean (value)	Percentage (%)	Mean (value)	Percentage (%)
Relationships	1444	16.2	1679	35.9	1310	21.4
Land expropriation and housing demolition	2805	31.4	249	5.3	915	14.9
Retirement and pension	3041	34.1	1174	25.1	1912	31.2
Insurance	1151	12.9	897	19.2	1298	21.2
Other	483	5.4	676	14.5	700	11.3
Income from transfer	8913	100.0	4675	100.0	6151	100.0

income are obvious. The median values of these two regions are both 1400 Yuan, however, illustrating that the gap is more severe in the east.

The internal structure of transfer income also has different features in different regions. In the east, rural households' transfer income comes primarily from retirement and pension income, compensation from land expropriation and housing demolition, and income from relationships, with mean values of 3041 Yuan, 2805 Yuan, and 1444 Yuan with percentages of 34.1, 31.4, and 16.2 %, respectively (see Table 3.16). The transfer income of rural households in the central region is comprised primarily of income from relationships, retirement and pension income, and insurance income with mean values of 1679 Yuan, 1174 Yuan, and 897 Yuan, accounting for 35.9, 25.1, and 19.2 %, respectively. Unlike the eastern region, compensation for land expropriation and housing demolition only comprises a small proportion of transfer income at 5.3 % in the central region (with the mean value being 249 Yuan). As for the western region, retirement and pension income, income from relationships, and insurance income constitute the majority of transfer income with mean values of 1912 Yuan, 1310 Yuan, and 1298 Yuan comprising 31.2, 21.4, and 21.2 %, respectively. Insurance income's makes up the highest percentage of total transfer income in the western region.

3.4 Income Disparity

According to Table 3.17, the total income level exceeded that of rural households in Q10, Q25, Q50, Q75, and Q90. This indicates that urban households generally earn higher incomes than rural households. At the same time, as the quantile increases, the income gap between rural China and the rest of the nation keeps widening. In addition, the standard deviation of total income of rural households is 83,817 Yuan, much lower than the total level. This shows that income disparity in the rural areas is smaller than in the urban areas.

Table 3.17 Distribution of total income of rural households (*unit* Yuan)

	Mean	Standard deviation	Quantile-10 (%)	Quantile-25 (%)	Quantile-50 (%)	Quantile-75 (%)	Quantile-90 (%)
Rural	36,560	83,817	2000	6500	20,900	47,160	82,680
Eastern	41,786	89,559	1635	6400	23,250	50,950	91,500
Central	35,046	84,067	2500	7300	21,500	47,100	82,200
Western	33,183	77,529	1825	5900	18,190	43,000	72,800
Overall	62,155	172,173	2600	11,850	36,000	72,350	127,800

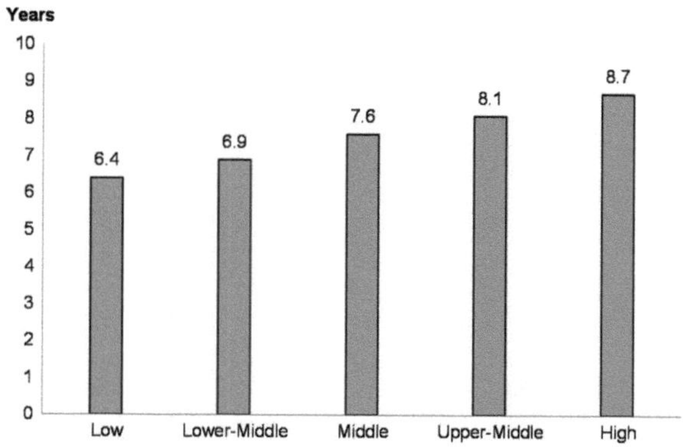

Chart 3.3 Income and years of education year of rural heads of households

Taking different regions into consideration, in Q10, the total income of eastern rural households was 1635 Yuan. This is 2500 Yuan lower than the central region and 1825 Yuan in the western region. In Q50, Q75, and Q90, however, the total income of eastern rural households are the highest of three regions, with a 18,700 Yuan disparity between the eastern and western regions in Q90. By the ratio of income in Q90 to Q10, the income disparity is more 56 times greater in eastern rural households. Compared to central and western rural households, the income disparities are 32.9 times and 39.9 times greater, respectively. Total income standard deviations are 89,559 Yuan, 84,067 Yuan, and 77,529 Yuan in eastern, central, and western China. This means that the income disparity in the east is significantly larger than in the central and western regions.

Chart 3.3 illustrates the relationship between the incomes rural households and heads of households' levels of education. In accordance with income level, rural households are divided into five groups in decreasing order: low, lower-middle, middle, upper-middle, and high income. It clearly shows that household income increases with the head of household's level of education. On average, heads of household with high incomes receive 8.7 years of education while those with low incomes only receive 6.4 years of education, a 2.3 year gap. Therefore, promoting educational equality serves as an important and effective means for bridging income disparity.

Chapter 4
Expenditures of Rural Households

In this chapter, rural household expenditure are divided by their purposes into three groups: agricultural production expenditures, consumption expenditures and transfer expenditures. The average numbers of these three groups are 9590 Yuan, 30,505 Yuan and 2645 Yuan, respectively. Statistics show that transfer expenditures exist in 75.0 % of rural households. Generally, 7.5 % of rural households' total income is spent on transfer expenditures, 2.2 % higher than urban households.

4.1 Agricultural Production Expenditures

The agricultural production expenditures of rural households are defined as expenditures for agricultural production and operation activities. It is mainly comprised of agricultural production costs and agricultural employment costs which are summarized in Table 4.1. As the table shows, rural households' production expenditures are 9590 Yuan with a 1140 Yuan median. The agricultural production cost is 9116 Yuan, accounting for 95.1 % of the total amount, and agricultural employment cost is 473 Yuan, accounting for 4.9 %. As a consequence, employment costs only constitute a small amount of agricultural production expenditures. Additionally, the median of employment cost is 0, indicating that most households do not have this cost.

Table 4.2 demonstrates agricultural production expenditures in different regions. In the eastern region, the average amount of agricultural production expenditures for rural households is 11,606 Yuan, with a median of 750 Yuan. In the central region, the average is 9763 Yuan while the median is 2000 Yuan. As for the western region, the average is 7516 Yuan and the median is 1000 Yuan. The eastern region has the highest mean values sequentially followed by the central and western regions. The median value, however, is highest in the central region followed by the western and eastern regions.

L. Gan et al., *Report on the Development of Household Finance in Rural China (2014)*, DOI 10.1007/978-981-10-0409-4_4

Table 4.1 Agricultural productive expenditure of rural households

Types of expenditure	Mean (Yuan)	Median (Yuan)	Percentage (%)
Agricultural production cost	9116	1000	95.1
Agricultural employment cost	473	0	4.9
Productive expenditure	9590	1140	100.0

Table 4.2 Agricultural productive expenditure of rural households in different regions (*unit* Yuan)

Types of expenditure	Eastern		Central		Western	
	Mean	Median	Mean	Median	Mean	Median
Production cost	10,825	700	9364	2000	7257	1000
Employment cost	781	0	399	0	259	0
Productive expenditure	11,606	750	9763	2000	7516	1000

Furthermore, all types of agricultural production expenditures and agricultural production and agricultural employment costs, are characterized by a decreasing trend from east to west.

4.2 Consumption Expenditures

4.2.1 Overview of Consumption Expenditures

Household consumption expenditures refer to expenditures in daily life on eight items, including expenses for food, clothing, residence, commodities and durables, healthcare and medical services, transportation and communication, education and entertainment, and other expenses.

A summary of rural households' consumption expenditures is illustrated in Table 4.3. The mean value of rural households' consumption expenditures is 30,505 Yuan and the median is 20,250 Yuan, both of which are far less than the total levels of 45,188 Yuan and 31,520 Yuan. Among total consumption expenditures of rural households, clothing expenses are 1526 Yuan; residence expenses are 6481 Yuan; commodity and durable expenses 2047 Yuan; healthcare and medical service expenses are 3325 Yuan; transportation and communication expenses are 3060 Yuan; education and entertainment expenses are 3566 Yuan; and other expenses are 435 Yuan. Lower consumption expenditures highlight the prominent standard of living differences between urban and rural households.

Chart 4.1 illustrates the consumption expenditures of rural Chinese households. As the chart shows, expenses for food, residence, and education and entertainment comprise the largest proportion with percentages of 33.0, 21.2, and 11.8 %, respectively, adding up to 66.0 %. It resembles the national situation in which three

Table 4.3 Consumption expenditures of rural households

Types of expenditures	Total		Rural	
	Mean	Median	Mean	Median
Food	15,818	12,000	10,073	6600
Clothing	2552	1000	1526	1000
Residence	8722	2726	6481	1200
Commodities and durables	3166	1200	2047	660
Healthcare and medical services	3630	1000	3352	1000
Transport and communications	4629	2160	3060	1440
Education and entertainment	6063	1240	3566	500
Other expenses	672	0	435	0
Consumption expenditure	45,188	31,520	30,505	20,250

afore mentioned expenses constitute 35.0, 19.3, and 13.4 %, respectively, forming the majority of consumption expenditures.

4.2.2 Consumption Expenditures and Income

Table 4.4 demonstrates the proportion of each type of consumption expenditure of the total household income.[1] For rural households, consumption expenditures comprise 83.5 % of total income, 10.3 % higher than the total level.

Statistics show that food expenses comprise 27.5 % of total rural household incomes; residence expenses comprise 17.7 %; healthcare and medical services comprise 9.2 %; education and entertainment comprise 9.7 %. Of this, expenses on food, residence, and healthcare and medical services all comprise larger portions than the total level. These three expenses are necessary daily expenses for households. The higher percentage in rural households reflects the fact that rural households face low incomes and a heavy burden of daily consumption and medical needs.

Rural household samples in this survey are divided into five groups in ascending order in accordance with their yearly after-tax income (all the figures excluded in the corresponding group): low-income households (less than 20 % of the total); lower-middle-income households (20–40 %); middle-income households (40–60 %); upper-middle-income households (60–80 %); and high-income

[1]Gross income of rural households is composed with agricultural income and non-agricultural income. The former refers to net income from agricultural production and operation activities, which equals to agricultural gross income minus agricultural production costs. The latter includes income from wages and salaries, business income, income from properties and transfer income. Business income, thereafter, is defined as the net income households obtain from industrial and business operation activities, including individual businesses and self-employed businesses.

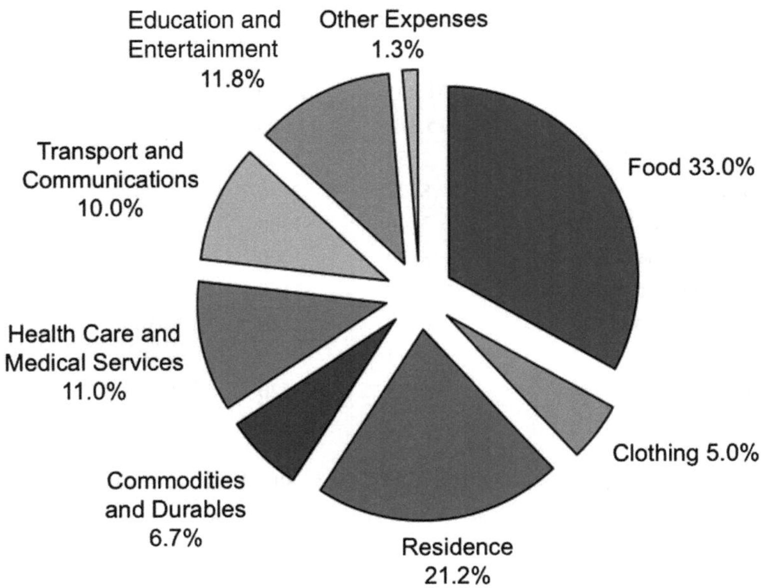

Chart 4.1 Composition of consumption expenditure of rural households

Table 4.4 Proportion of types of expenditure in total income (*unit %*)

	Total	Rural
Food	25.6	27.5
Clothing	4.1	4.2
Residence	14.1	17.7
Commodities and durables	5.1	5.6
Healthcare and medical services	5.9	9.2
Transport and communications	7.5	8.4
Education and entertainment	9.8	9.7
Other expenses	1.1	1.2
Consumption expenditure	73.2	83.5

households (80–100 %). Table 4.5 illustrates the consumption expenditure structure in different rural households.

It is clear that expenses on food, housing, and transportation and communications take up the majority of consumption expenditures in rural households with high incomes. Transportation and communication expenses in particular have become a major part of consumption expenditures for high-income rural households, accounting for 13.3 % and is significantly higher than other households. Additionally, higher food and clothing expenses for high-income rural households indicate that they focus more on high-quality foods.

Table 4.5 Consumption expenditure structure of rural households with different income (*unit* %)

Types of expenditures	Low	Lower-middle	Middle	Upper-middle	High
Food	29.6	33.9	36.0	33.1	32.3
Clothing	4.9	4.2	4.9	5.1	6.3
Residence	20.8	21.4	18.9	23.9	21.6
Commodities and durables	7.5	5.7	6.0	7.9	6.8
Healthcare and medical services	13.2	12.3	11.6	8.8	7.8
Transport and communications	10.5	9.1	8.8	9.1	13.3
Education and entertainment	12.8	12.3	12.2	10.5	10.1
Other expenses	0.7	1.1	1.6	1.6	1.8
Total	100.0	100.0	100.0	100.0	100.0

As for the remaining four groups, expenses on food, housing, and healthcare and medical service form the majority. As a result, most households face a heavy burden out of medical needs, especially lower-middle-income and low-income households whose healthcare and medical service expenses are 12.3 and 13.2 %, respectively. In addition, the education and entertainment expenses of lower-middle-income households have risen to more than 10 % of the total, a higher percentage than upper-middle-income and high-income households. Such a large proportion, however, does not result from these households' excessive spending but from the huge demand and income shortage dilemma.

4.2.3 Regional Disparities in Consumption Expenditures

Table 4.6 illustrates the consumption expenditures of rural households in different regions. The annual consumption expenditures and mean value are 35,242 Yuan and 22,455 Yuan in the eastern region; 27,745 Yuan and 18,920 Yuan in the central

Table 4.6 Consumption expenditure of rural households in different regions (*unit* Yuan)

Types of expenditure	Eastern		Central		Western	
	Mean	Median	Mean	Median	Mean	Median
Food	11,858	7500	8829	6090	9658	6450
Clothing	1772	1000	1457	1000	1371	800
Residence	8083	1800	5723	1080	5745	1140
Commodities and durables	2463	720	1740	660	1969	720
Healthcare and medical services	3216	750	3205	1000	3630	1200
Transport and communication	3593	1560	2584	1200	3043	1500
Education and entertainment	3889	400	3725	500	3100	450
Other expenses	434	0	516	0	353	0
Consumption expenditure	35,242	22,455	27,745	18,920	28,853	19,980

Table 4.7 Composition of consumption expenditures of rural households in different regions (*unit* %)

Types of expenditures	Eastern	Central	Western
Food	33.6	31.8	33.5
Clothing	5.0	5.3	4.8
Residence	22.9	20.6	19.9
Commodities and durables	7.0	6.3	6.8
Healthcare and medical services	9.1	11.6	12.6
Transport and communication	10.2	9.3	10.5
Education and entertainment	11.0	13.4	10.7
Other expenses	1.2	1.7	1.2
Total	100.0	100.0	100.0

region; and 28,853 Yuan and 19,980 Yuan in the western region. Therefore, consumption expenditures are the highest in the eastern region and the lowest in the central region.

Table 4.7 shows the composition of the consumption expenditures of rural households in different regions. According to the data, expenses on food, housing, education and entertainment, and healthcare and medical services comprise the majority of consumption expenditures in all three regions. The four aforementioned types of expenditures vary significantly among different regions. For western rural households, healthcare and medical service expenses comprise the largest proportion at 12.6 %. Meanwhile, for eastern rural households, residence expenses comprise the majority at 22.9 %. It is noteworthy that education and entertainment expenses comprise 13.4 % of total consumption expenditures for rural households in the central regions. This is obviously higher than those in the eastern or western regions.

In general, households in different regions bear diverse consumption features. Rural households in the eastern region spend most of their consumption expenditures on housing and commodities and durable expenses; rural households in the central region spend more on clothing and education and entertainment; and rural households in the western region spend more on healthcare and medical services.

4.3 Transfer Expenditures

4.3.1 Overview of Transfer Expenditures

Transfer expenditures refers to cash or non-cash contributions provided for people or organizations outside of the household members, including contributions during holidays such as Spring Festival and the Mid-autumn Festival, wedding and funeral expenditures, expenditures on education, healthcare, and accommodation subsidies, or other expenditures.

Table 4.8 Transfer expenditures of rural households

Expenditure item	Overall		Rural	
	Mean (Yuan)	Percentage (%)	Mean (Yuan)	Percentage (%)
Holiday expenditures	1166	31.9	633	23.9
Wedding and funeral expenditures	1763	48.2	1604	60.6
Education/healthcare/accommodation expenditures	634	17.3	370	14.0
Other expenditures	96	2.6	38	1.5
Transfer expenditures	3659	100.0	2645	100.0

The CHFS data suggests that 75 % of rural households in China have transfer expenditures, and that an average 7.5 % of their total income is spent on transfer expenditures, 2.2 % higher than urban households.

Table 4.8 shows the transfer expenditures of rural households in China. The transfer expenditures per rural household are 2654 Yuan, 1014 Yuan lower than the overall per household transfer expenditures. Among them, holiday expenditures, wedding and funeral expenditures, education/health care/accommodation expenditures, and other expenditures are 633 Yuan, 1604 Yuan, 370 Yuan, and 38 Yuan, respectively, and account for 23.9, 60.6, 14.0, and 1.4 %, respectively. This suggests that the transfer expenditures of rural Chinese households are mainly spent on weddings and funerals, 12.4 % higher than overall households.

Transfer expenditures can be divided into four categories according to its recipients: parents, parents-in-law, other relatives, and non-relatives. Chart 4.2

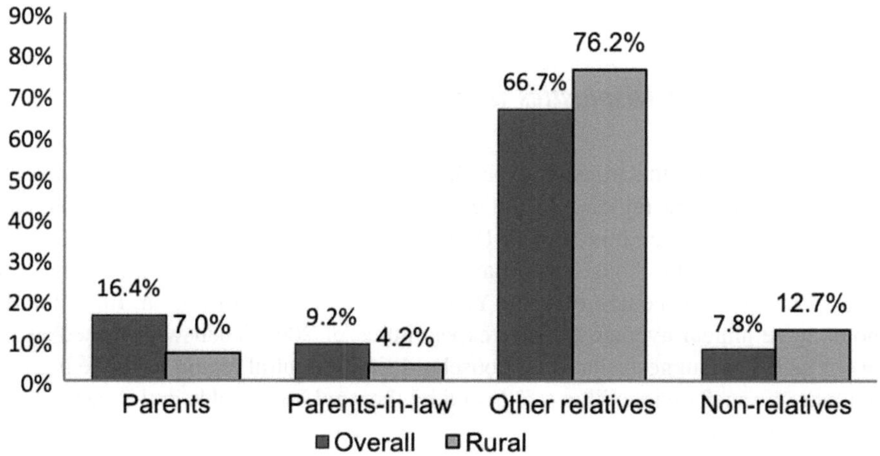

Chart 4.2 Household transfer expenditure based on expenditure objectives

shows the statistical results of the transfer expenditures of rural households in China grouped by recipient. As Chart 4.2 shows, transfer expenditures on other relatives comprise the largest portion, 66.7 % of total transfer expenditures. In rural households, the transfer expenditures on other relatives account for a much larger proportion, comprising 76.2, 10.5 % larger than overall households. In addition, 7.0 % of the transfer expenditures of rural households is spent on parents and 4.2 % on parents-in-law. It is noteworthy that the proportion of transfer expenditures by rural households for non-relatives is not low and accounts for 12.7, 4.9 % higher than overall households. In a word, the transfer expenditures of rural households to other relatives and non-relatives jointly accounted for 88.9 %. This suggests that rural people pay more attention to social relationships than urban people.

Table 4.9 shows the structure of transfer expenditures of rural households in China based on income classification. We sort the rural households survey samples into five groups from low to high in accordance with the annual household after-tax income levels (all figures excluded in corresponding group): low-income households (20 % of the lowest income); lower-middle-income households (20–40 % of the lowest income); middle-income households (40–60 % of the lowest income); upper-middle-income households (20–40 % of the highest income); and high-income households (20 % of the highest income).

Table 4.9 illustrates that wedding and funeral expenditures account for the highest proportion of transfer expenditure for rural households regardless of income level and is particularly prominent in middle-income households, accounting for 63.9 %. The largest proportion of holiday expenditures occurs in upper-middle-income households, accounting for 26.3 %. Additionally, the education/health care/accommodation expenditures of upper-middle-income households and high-income households comprise larger proportions at 15.9 and 16.4 %, respectively.

4.3.2 Regional Disparities in Transfer Expenditures

Table 4.10 shows the transfer expenditures of rural households in the eastern, central, and western regions. In the eastern region, rural households have annual average transfer expenditures of 2818 Yuan with a median of 1000 Yuan; in the central region, rural households have annual average transfer expenditures of 3054 Yuan with a median of 1500 Yuan; and in the western region, rural households have annual average transfer expenditures of 2067 Yuan with a median of 900 Yuan. This suggests that rural households in the central region have the highest amount of transfer expenditures followed by the rural households in the eastern and western regions.

Table 4.9 The structure of transfer expenditures of rural household based on income levels (*unit %*)

Expenditure items	Low-income	Lower-middle-income	Middle-income	Upper-middle-income	High-income
Holiday expenditures	24.7	22.7	22.8	26.3	23.7
Wedding and funeral expenditures	62.5	61.9	63.9	55.8	58.1
Education/healthcare/accommodation expenditures	11.6	14.2	12.2	15.9	16.4
Other expenditures	1.2	1.2	1.1	2.0	1.8

Table 4.10 Transfer expenditures of rural households in eastern, central and western regions

Expenditure items	Households in eastern region		Households in central region		Households in western region	
	Mean (Yuan)	Percentage (%)	Mean (Yuan)	Percentage (%)	Mean (Yuan)	Percentage (%)
Holiday expenditures	768	27.3	701	23.0	439	21.2
Wedding and funeral expenditures	1536	54.5	1865	61.1	1405	68.0
Education/healthcare/accommodation expenditures	444	15.8	458	15.0	210	10.2
Other expenditures	71	2.4	31	0.9	13	0.6
Transfer expenditures	2818	100.0	3054	100.0	2067	100.0

We find that the expenditure structures of rural households in different regions have different characteristics. The holiday expenditures and education/health care/accommodation expenditures of rural households in the eastern region are higher than those of rural households in the central and western regions, accounting for 27.3 and 15.8 %, respectively. Rural households in the western region spend relatively more on wedding and funeral expenditures.

Chapter 5
Rural Household Properties

This chapter describes the property of rural households from three aspects, including rural household assets, debts, and net assets. By analyzing the statistics, we find that the average rural household has 317,200 Yuan in assets, but only 23.7 % of households' total assets reach the mean level. The average value of rural household debts is 21,600 Yuan and 295,000 Yuan of net assets. With the unbalanced property distribution of rural households, the richest 10 % of households possess 54 % of all rural household properties.

5.1 Rural Household Assets

Household assets consist of non-financial and financial assets. Household non-financial assets include agricultural and business operation assets, land and real estate, and vehicles and durable assets. Household financial assets include cash, demand deposits, time deposits, social security account balances, stocks, bonds, funds, derivatives, wealth management products, non-RMB assets, gold, loans to others, etc.

5.1.1 Overview of Rural Household Assets

By July 2013, rural households have 317,200 Yuan in assets with a median of 132,700 Yuan. Table 5.1 illustrates the regional distribution of total assets of rural households. The assets per rural household in the eastern region are 432,200 Yuan with a median of 170,000 Yuan, higher than the average value of overall household assets. In the central region, the average rural household has 244,300 Yuan in assets with a median of 122,000 Yuan. In the western region, rural households have average assets of 283,500 Yuan with a median of 114,200 Yuan. Rural household

L. Gan et al., *Report on the Development of Household Finance in Rural China (2014)*, DOI 10.1007/978-981-10-0409-4_5

Table 5.1 Regional disparity of rural households assets (*unit* Yuan)

Region	Mean	Median
Eastern	432,200	170,000
Central	244,300	122,000
Western	283,500	114,200
Rural	317,200	132,700

Table 5.2 Interval distribution of total assets of rural households

Asset interval	Percentage (%)
Below 45,000 Yuan	25.0
45,000–133,000 Yuan	25.0
133,000–317,000 Yuan	26.3
317,000–1 million Yuan	18.3
1 million–10 million Yuan	5.2
More than 10 million Yuan	0.2

assets in the eastern region are significantly higher than the central and western regions. The average value of rural household assets in the central region and the median rural household assets in the western region rank the lowest.

Table 5.2 shows the interval distribution of the total assets of rural households in China. As the data shows, 25.0 % of rural households have less than 45,000 Yuan in total assets; 25.0 % of rural households have total assets of 45,000–133,000 Yuan; 26.3 % of rural households have total assets of 133,000–317,000 Yuan; 18.3 % of rural households have total assets of 317,000–1,000,000 Yuan; 5.2 % of rural households have total assets of 1–10 million Yuan group; and 0.2 % of rural households have more than 10 million Yuan in total assets. Less than 25 % of rural households' total assets reach the average level.

5.1.2 *The Structure of Rural Household Assets*

5.1.2.1 Financial Assets and Non-financial Assets

Table 5.3 shows the structure of rural household assets. Rural households have an average of 317,200 Yuan in assets, including 23,200 Yuan in financial assets and 294,100 Yuan in non-financial assets, accounting for 7.0 and 93.0 % of total assets, respectively. This shows that most rural household assets are non-financial assets.

Table 5.3 Financial assets and non-financial assets of rural households (*unit* Yuan)

Composition of assets	Mean	Median
Non-financial assets	294,100	117,100
Financial assets	23,200	3,000
Total assets	317,200	132,700

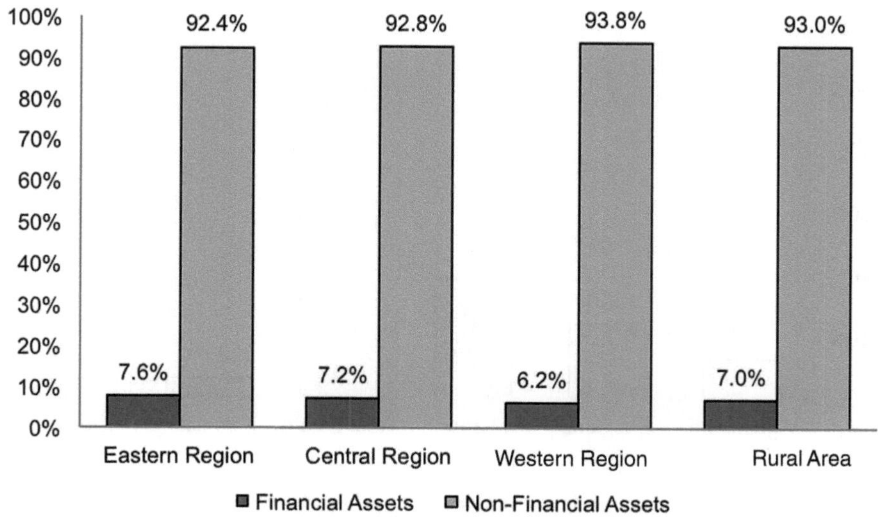

Chart 5.1 The structure of rural household assets in different regions

Rural households' proportion of financial assets is 3.3 % lower than urban households.

Chart 5.1 compares the regional disparities of the structure of rural household assets. The financial and non-financial assets of rural households are 7.6 and 92.4 % in the eastern region, respectively; 7.2 and 92.8 % in the central region; and 6.2 and 93.8 % in the western region. This suggests that the proportion of financial assets of rural households decreases progressively from the east to the west.

5.1.2.2 Non-financial Assets

Non-financial assets include agricultural assets (machinery), business assets, land, real estate, vehicles, and durables. As Chart 5.2 shows, among rural households' non-financial assets, agricultural assets account for 6.3 %, business assets comprise 12.0 %, land comprises 18.9 %, real estate comprises 57.0 %, vehicles comprise 3.0 %, and durables comprise 2.8 %. This implies that the non-financial assets of rural households are mainly embodied as real estate and land. Combined, they account for 75.9 %.

5.1.2.3 Financial Assets

Financial assets include cash, demand deposits, time deposits, social security account balances, stocks, bonds, funds, derivatives, wealth management products, non-RMB assets, gold, loans to others etc. Chart 5.3 shows the proportion of all

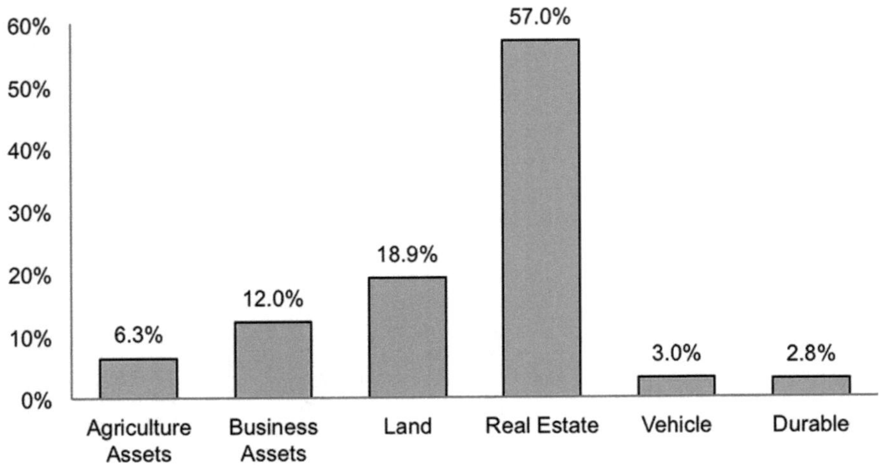

Chart 5.2 Composition of non-financial assets of rural households

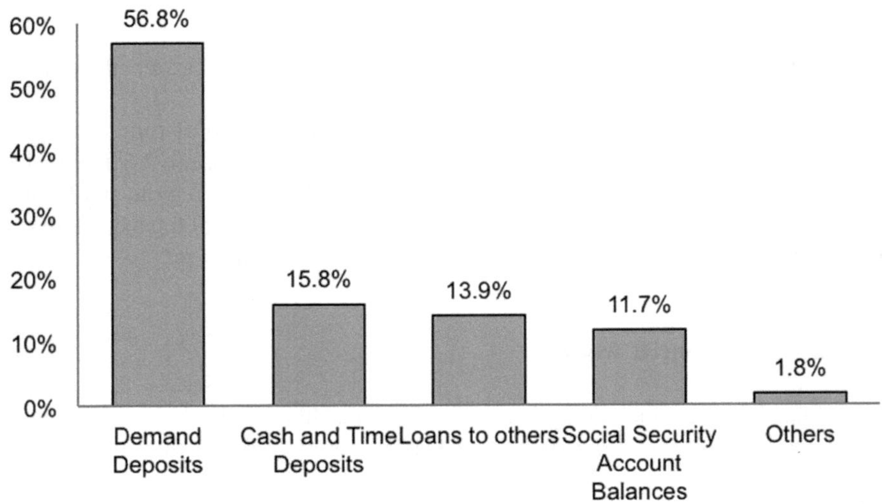

Chart 5.3 Composition of financial assets of rural households

financial assets. Among the financial assets of rural households, demand deposits account for 56.8 %, cash and time deposits account for 15.8 %, loans to others account for 13.9 %, and social security account balances comprise 11.7 %. This shows that the financial assets of rural households are mainly embodied as cash and deposits.

The financial assets shall be divided into risk-free assets and risk assets according to their risk attributes. Risk-free assets include cash, demand deposits, time deposits, treasury bonds, municipal bonds, stock account balances and social

Table 5.4 The proportion of risk-free assets and risk assets of rural households

Area	Risk assets (%)	Risk-free assets (%)
Rural	15.6	84.4
Overall	24.1	75.9

security account balances, etc. Risk assets include stocks, funds, financial bonds, enterprises bonds, financial derivatives, wealth management products, non-RMB assets, gold and loans to others, etc.

As Table 5.4 shows, rural households' financial risk assets account for 15.6 % and risk-free assets account for 84.4 %. Rural households prefer risk-free assets, 8.5 % higher than overall households.

5.1.3 The Value of Real Estate and Agricultural Machinery of Rural Households

5.1.3.1 Real Estate

Chart 5.4 compares the home-ownership rates of rural households among different regions. Overall, the rural household home-ownership rate is 92.9 % and the home-ownership rate varies little among rural households across the eastern, central, and western regions, accounting for 92.1, 94.0, and 92.6 %, respectively.

Table 5.5 shows that the mean value of rural households' real estate is 183,500 Yuan with a median value of 80,000 Yuan. From a regional perspective, the mean and median values of real estate of rural households are 269,800 and 100,000 Yuan in the

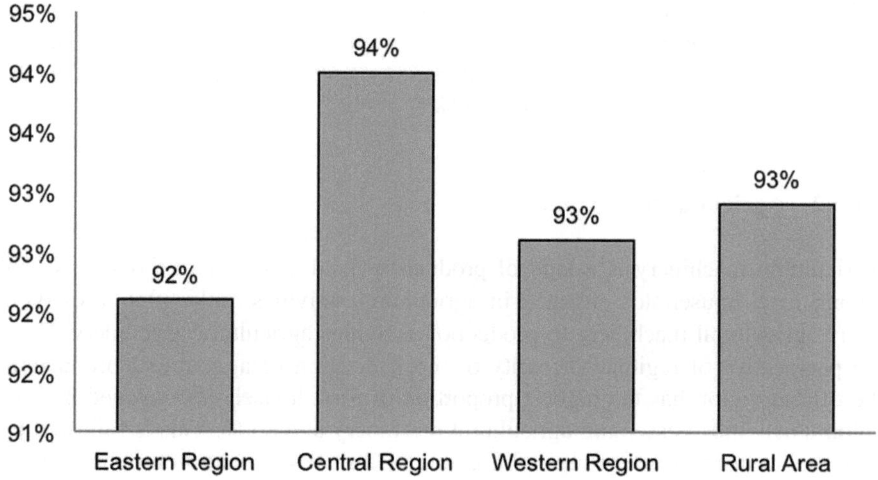

Chart 5.4 Regional disparity of the home-ownership rate of rural households

Table 5.5 The value of real estate of rural households (*unit* Yuan)

Region	Mean	Median
Eastern	269,800	100,000
Central	136,800	65,000
Western	151,300	60,000
Rural area	183,500	80,000

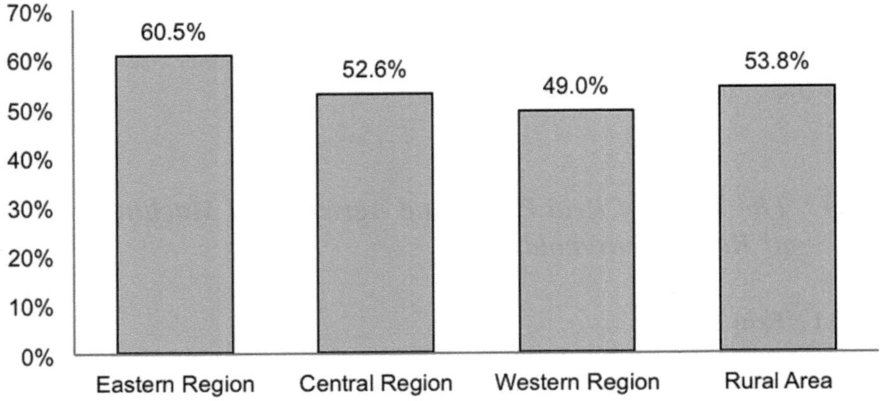

Chart 5.5 The proportion of real estate of rural households assets

eastern region; 136,800 and 65,000 Yuan in the central region; and 151,300 and 60,000 Yuan in the western region. The value of the real estate of rural households in the eastern region is much higher than in the central and western regions.

Chart 5.5 compares the proportionate disparity of the real estate of rural households in different regions. Real estate accounts for 53.8 % of total rural household assets. From a regional perspective, real estate comprises the largest proportion of rural household assets in the eastern region, accounting for 60.5 %, followed by households in the central region at 52.6 % and households in the western region have the lowest at 49.0 %.

5.1.3.2 Agricultural Machinery

Agricultural machinery is a kind of productive fixed asset. Chart 5.6 shows, that among rural households engaged in agricultural activities, only 39.9 % of them apply agricultural machinery to production activities agricultural machinery. From the perspective of regional disparity of mechanization of agricultural production, the central region has the highest proportion of rural households engaged in agricultural activities possessing agricultural machinery at 44.5 %. This is followed by households in the western region, accounting for 39.6 %, and households in the eastern region with the lowest at 34.1 %.

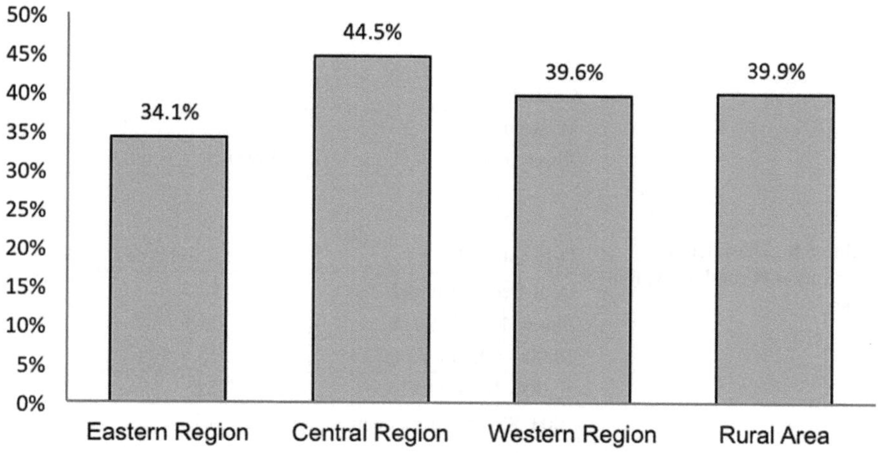

Chart 5.6 The proportion of rural households possessing agricultural machinery

Table 5.6 Regional disparity of the value of agricultural machinery of rural households (*unit* Yuan)

Regional distribution	Mean	Median
Eastern	7,807	1,600
Central	8,740	2,500
Western	5,314	1,500
Rural area	7,340	2,000

From a perspective of the value of agricultural machinery, there is a large value span in agricultural machinery of rural households. About 17 % of rural households engaged in agricultural activities possess agricultural machinery that is worth more than 10,000 Yuan and about 37 % possess agricultural machinery that is worth less than 1000 Yuan. From the perspective of the median value of agricultural machinery, the median is 2000 Yuan for rural households possessing agricultural machinery. The median value of agricultural machinery in the eastern and western regions are 1600 Yuan and 1500 Yuan, respectively. The median in the central region is 2500 Yuan. From the perspective of the mean value of agricultural machinery, the mean is 7340 Yuan for rural households possessing agricultural machinery. The mean value of agricultural machinery is 7807 Yuan in the eastern region, 8740 Yuan in the central region, and 5314 Yuan in the western region (see Table 5.6).

5.2 Rural Household Debts

Rural household debts include agricultural and business loans, housing loans, vehicle loans, financial investment loans, credit card loans, education loans, and others.

Table 5.7 Regional disparity of rural household debts (*unit* Yuan)

Regional distribution	Mean	Median
Eastern	22,100	0
Central	20,200	0
Western	22,400	0
Rural area	21,600	0

Table 5.8 The interval distribution of rural household debts

Debt intervals	Rural area (%)
Debt-free households	62.3
Below 10,000 Yuan	11.6
10,000–50,000 Yuan	15.5
50,000–100,000 Yuan	5.8
100,000–1 million Yuan	4.7
More than 1 million Yuan	0.1
Total	100

5.2.1 *Overview of Rural Household Debts*

Table 5.7 shows the regional disparity of rural household debts. The debt per rural household in China is 21,600 Yuan. The debt per rural household in the eastern region is 22,100 Yuan with a median of 0 Yuan; the debts per rural household in the central region is 20,200 Yuan with a median of 0 Yuan; and the debt per rural household in the western region is 22,400 Yuan with a median of 0 Yuan. Rural household debt in the western region is higher than the eastern and central regions. Rural household debts in the central region are relatively low.

As Table 5.8 shows, 62.3 % of rural households do not have debts. That means that 37.7 % of rural households do have debt, 6.9 % more than indebted urban households. 11.6 % of rural households have less than 10,000 Yuan in debt; 15.5 % of rural households have 10,000–50,000 Yuan in debt; 5.8 % of rural households have 50,000–100,000 Yuan in debt; 4.7 % of rural households have 100,000–1,000,000 Yuan in debt; and 0.1 % of rural households have more than 1 million Yuan in debt.

5.2.2 *The Structure of Rural Households Debts*

Chart 5.7 shows five major sources of rural household debts, including housing debts; agricultural and business debts; education debts; other debts; and vehicle debts. Housing debts comprise 40.0 %; agricultural and business debts comprise 33.6 %; education debts comprise 6.0 %; other debts comprise 15.0 %; and vehicle debts comprise 5.4 %. This shows that half of rural household debt is housing debts.

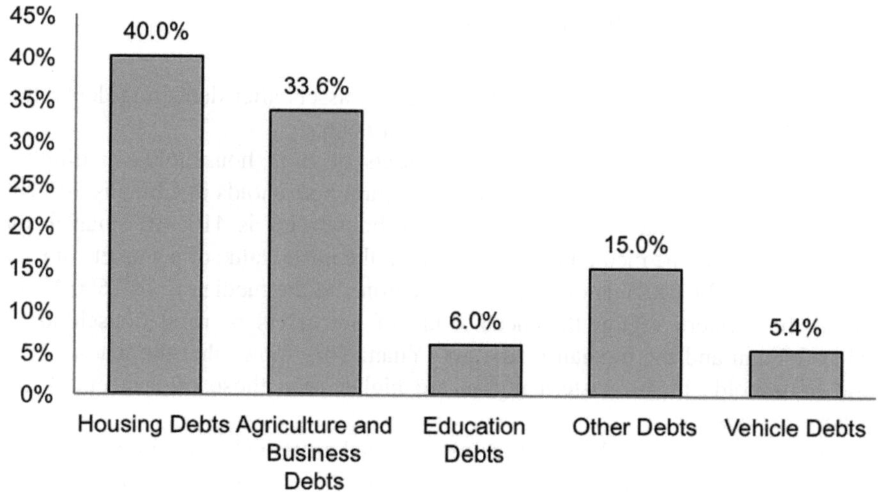

Chart 5.7 The composition of rural household debts

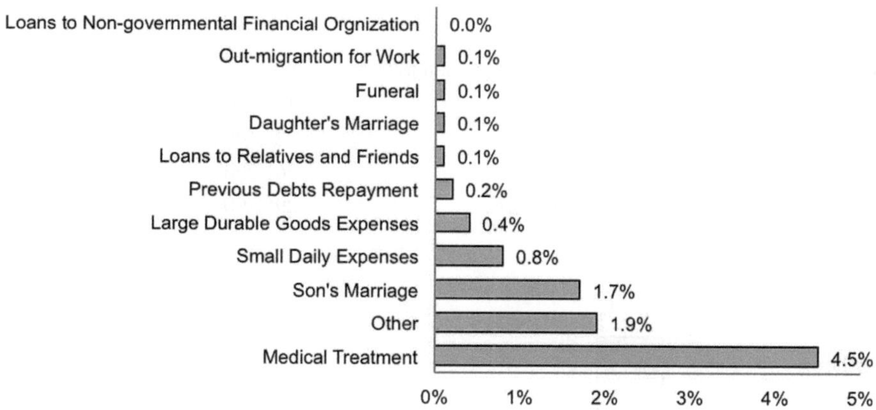

Chart 5.8 Reasons for other debts of rural households

Chart 5.8 shows the other rural household debts. From Chart 5.8, we see that the main sources of other rural household debts are medical treatment, other debts, sons' marriage, and small daily expenses. 4.5 % of rural households are in debt for medical treatment, and only 1.5 % of urban households are in debt because of medical treatment. 37.7 % of rural households have debt and this means that 11.9 % of rural households are in debt for medical treatment. This suggests that the rural medical insurance levels should be further enhanced. 1.7 % of rural households are in debt for sons' marriages, and 0.1 % of rural households are in debt for loans to relatives. Only a few rural households borrow money from non-governmental financial organizations in order to lend money to others.

5.3 Net Assets of Rural Households

Net assets of rural households refer to household assets after deducting debts; that is, the difference between total assets and total debts.

Table 5.9 shows the disparity of net assets of rural households in different regions. As Table 5.9 shows, the net assets of rural households in China is 295,700 Yuan. The mean value of net assets of rural households is 410,100 Yuan in the eastern region and the median is 158,600 Yuan; the mean value of net assets of rural households is 224,100 Yuan in the central region and the median is 107,600 Yuan; and in the western region the mean value of net assets of rural households is 261,200 Yuan and the median is 104,600 Yuan. This shows that the net assets of rural households in the eastern region are higher than those of the central and western regions.

Household net asset values include net financial assets value, net house property value, net land value, net vehicle value, net productive fixed asset values, durable goods, and other debts. Chart 5.9 shows the structure of net assets of rural households. Net house property value accounts for 54 % and is the main component of rural households' net assets.

Table 5.9 Regional distribution of net assets of rural households (*unit* Yuan)

Regional distribution	Mean	Median
Eastern	410,100	158,600
Central	224,100	107,600
Western	261,200	104,600
Rural area	295,700	118,300

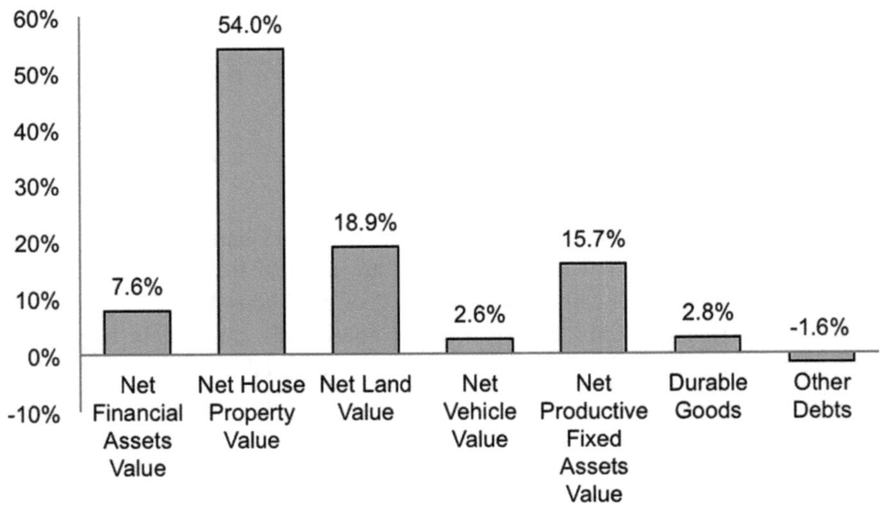

Chart 5.9 The structure of net assets of rural households

Table 5.10 Interval distribution of net assets of rural households

Interval distribution	Rural area (%)
Below 0 Yuan	4.0
0–36,400 Yuan	21.0
36,400–118,300 Yuan	25.0
118,300–593,200 Yuan	40.0
593,200–1 million Yuan	5.0
1 million–10 million Yuan	4.8
More than 10 million Yuan	0.2
Total	100

As Table 5.10 shows, 4.0 % of households have less than 0 Yuan in net assets (negative net worth); 21.0 % of households have 0–36,400 Yuan in net assets; 25.0 % of households have net assets of 36,400–118,300 Yuan; 40.0 % of households have 118,300–593,200 Yuan in net assets; 5.0 % of households have 593,200–1 million Yuan in net assets; 4.8 % of households have 1–10 million Yuan in net assets; and 0.2 % of households have more than 10 million Yuan in net assets.

5.4 Wealth Disparity of Rural Households

Presently, economic inequality arouses public attention. Economic inequality has two meanings: income disparity and household wealth disparity. This section performs an in-depth analysis of the wealth distribution of rural households in China. Household wealth refers to net assets and equals the total assets after deducting debts.

This section adopts the quartering method to analyze the unequal distribution of household wealth; this means that this method sorts household wealth from low to high into four quartered groups. Chart 5.10 shows the disparity in the mean values of net assets between rural and urban households. As Chart 5.10 shows, there is large disparity in the net assets between rural and urban households. The poorest 25 % of rural households have 4800 Yuan in net assets and the poorest 25 % of urban households have a mean value of 34,500 Yuan in net assets. The mean value of the poorest rural households (lower than quantile-25 %) only accounts for 13.9 % of that of the poorest urban households. Among rural households with highest wealth (higher than quantile-75 %), the mean value of net assets is 915,300 Yuan and the mean value of net assets of urban households with highest wealth is 3.1705 million Yuan. The former's mean value (lower than quantile-25 %) only accounts for 28.7 % of the latter's. There is still serious household wealth disparity among rural households. Rural households with the highest amounts of net assets have net worth 191.3 times higher than rural households with the lowest net assets. Urban households with highest net assets are only 91.9 times wealthier than the urban households with the least net assets.

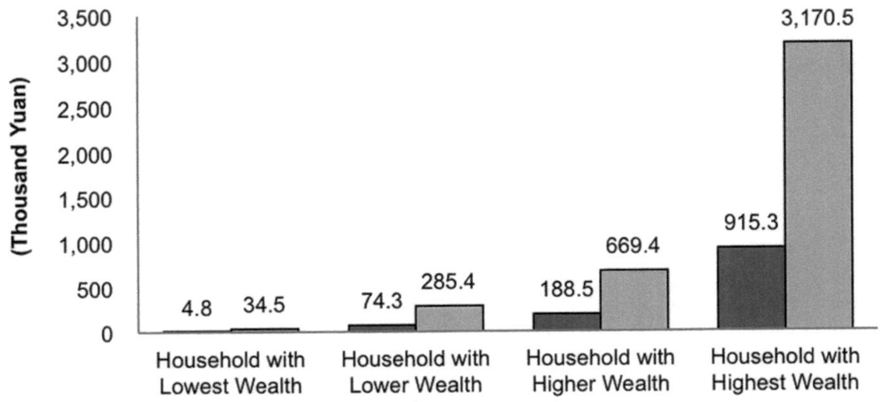

Chart 5.10 Disparity of the mean value of net assets betweeen rural and urban households

Table 5.11 Distribution of net wealth of rural households

Decile group (from low to high)	Percentage of net assets (%)
1	–
2	0.6
3	1.3
4	2.2
5	3.4
6	4.9
7	6.9
8	9.8
9	15.4
10	54

Table 5.11 illustrates the distribution of rural household wealth which is equally divided into decile groups. The numbers in Table 5.10 represent the percentage of net assets of households in each group, clearly reflecting the wealth disparity among rural households. Table 5.11 shows that the wealthiest 10 % of rural households possess 54 % of total rural wealth and the total wealth of the poorest 10 % of rural household is negative. This means that there is an insolvency problem. In addition, the wealthiest 20 % of rural households possess nearly 70 % of the rural wealth.

Chapter 6
Current Development Status of the Rural Financial Market

The rural financial market is important for rural economic development. For important participants in financial market (rural households), the development of the rural financial market not only relates to preserving and increasing wealth, but also to whether they can obtain adequate credit funds to change the initial endowment and expand sources of income to improve earnings. Based on the CHFS statistics (2013), this chapter introduces the status of China's rural financial market, including the rural risk market, rural credit market, rural finance, and household consumption. According to the analysis, the development of the rural financial market still lags behind; the participation rate of rural households in the stock and fund markets stands at a low rate, far below the overall participation rate; rural households' participation in the formal credit market also stands at a low rate with small disparities compared with the overall participation rate; and rural households participate actively in the private lending market which shows that private loans can be a sound supplement for formal loans. As for consumption, with modern finance increasingly penetrating consumption, the patterns of modern consumption like non-cash payment, credit cards, online shopping, and others have begun to influence rural households' consumption behavior. The modernization level of rural households' consumption pattern still lags behind the overall modernization level.

6.1 Risk Market

6.1.1 Overview of Household Participation in the Risk Market

CHFS creates surveys on a number of households' risk assets, including stocks, funds, bonds, wealth management products, financial derivatives, non-RMB assets,

L. Gan et al., *Report on the Development of Household Finance in Rural China (2014)*, DOI 10.1007/978-981-10-0409-4_6

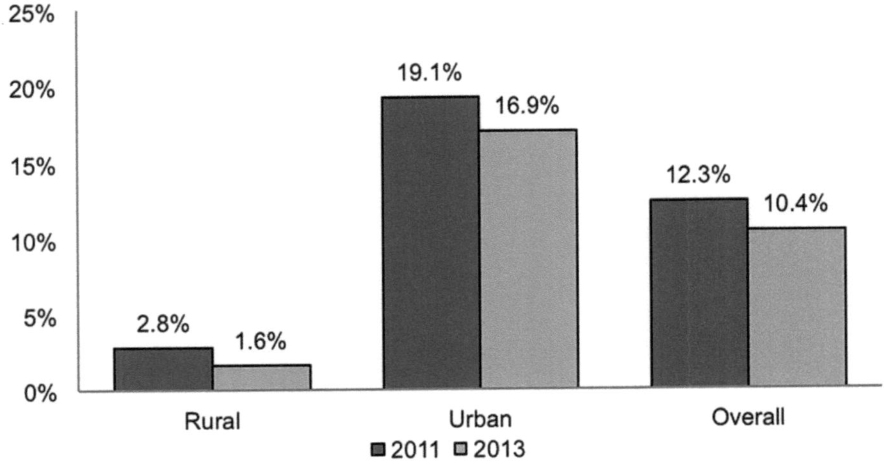

Chart 6.1 The participation rate of households in risk markets

and gold. If a household possesses one or more of any the above-mentioned risk assets, it will be deemed as participating in the risk market.

Recently, there has been an economic downturn domestically and abroad and all kinds of risk markets are frustrated, weakening the households' participation in risk markets. As shown in Chart 6.1, the proportion of households' participation in the risk market fell in 2013 compared to 2011. The proportion of rural households' participation in risk markets is far below that of overall and urban households. In 2013, the rural household participation rate was only 1.6, 10.4 % of all households, and 19.6 % of urban households. Rural households' participation rate was only approximately 10 % of that of urban households. This shows that the participation rate of households involved in China's risk markets is generally low and only a few rural households participate in risk markets. Therefore, we should further improve the financial markets and increase the market's vitality.

6.1.2 Comparison of Household Participation in All Kinds of Risk Markets

As shown in Table 6.1, from an annual perspective, the participation rate of rural households in the stock and funds markets dropped from 1.2 and 0.7 % in 2011 to 0.4 and 0.4 % in 2013, respectively. This may result from limited financial capability and weak risk resistance capability. Considering past stock market and funds market fluctuations, rural households have a higher tendency to withdraw from the markets. Judging from the overall level, the participation rates are different in

Table 6.1 Household participation in various risk markets (*unit* %)

	2011			2013		
	Rural	Urban	Overall	Rural	Urban	Overall
Stock market	1.2	13.8	8.6	0.4	11.0	6.5
Funds market	0.7	6.6	4.2	0.4	5.2	3.1
Bonds market	0.4	0.8	0.6	0.2	1.1	0.7
Wealth management product market	0.2	1.7	1.0	0.1	3.0	1.8
Non-RMB asset market	0.5	2.2	1.5	0.2	1.5	0.9
Gold market	0.4	0.7	0.6	0.4	1.3	0.9

various markets. The participation rates of households involved in the stocks, funds and non-RMB assets market have fallen while there have been increases in all other markets. The participation rates of households involved in wealth management products market increased from 1 to 1.8 %, showing that all major banks have strove to develop wealth management products in recent years and exert sound influence. The participation rate of households involved in the gold market has risen significantly from 0.6 to 0.9 %. This conforms to the gold fever over the past two years.

From the perspective of rural and urban areas, the participation rate of rural households in all kinds of risk markets is far below that of overall households. The 2013 numbers show that the participation rates of rural households in all kinds of risk markets are all lower than 0.5 %. The figure is much higher for overall households and urban households. Take the stock markets as an example; the participation rate of rural households is 0.4 % while overall households and urban households are 6 and 10 % higher than rural households, respectively. This suggests that the development of rural risk markets is far behind.

6.2 Credit Market

6.2.1 Loans Market

6.2.1.1 General Situation of Household Participation in Loans Market

Compared with 2011, the proportion of rural, urban, and overall households carrying loans rose slightly in 2013 from 13.9, 14.9, and 14.5 to 14.1, 15.9, and 15.1 %, respectively. The disparity between rural and urban households is not significant. Generally, the development of rural households' involvement in the loans market does not largely lag behind the overall and urban households (Chart 6.2).

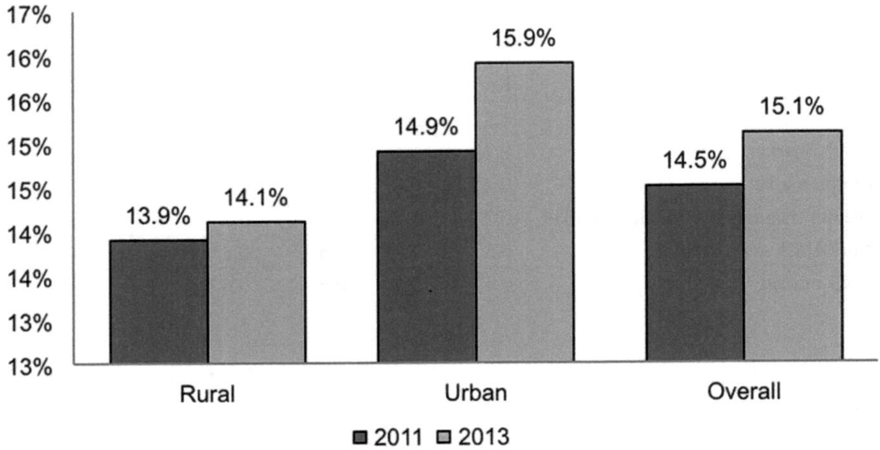

Chart 6.2 The proportion of households carrying loans in 2011 and 2013

6.2.1.2 Loans of Households

For the purposes of this paper, loans can be divided into five categories: production and operation loans; housing loans; automobile loans; education loans; and other loans. As shown in Table 6.2, from an annual perspective, the proportion of various loans that rural and urban households carry change over two years. The proportion of production and operation loans and education loans of rural households increased. This means that more and more rural households can obtain capital from formal credit to improve their incomes from production and operation activities and ease their educational burdens. The proportion of housing loans and others decreased slightly and the proportion of automobile loans generally stayed the same. From the perspective of overall household loans, the proportion of production and operation loans, education loans, and automobile loans all increased while housing loans and other loans dropped slightly.

As shown in Chart 6.3, the proportion of production loans, education loans and other loans of rural households was significantly higher than for urban and overall households. Rural households have a much lower proportion of housing loans than

Table 6.2 Participation of households in loans markets (*unit %*)

	2011			2013		
	Rural	Urban	Overall	Rural	Urban	Overall
Production and operation loans	5.7	2.1	3.6	6.2	2.4	4.0
Housing loans	5.5	11.3	8.9	4.9	11.7	8.8
Automobile loans	1.0	1.3	1.2	1.0	1.8	1.4
Education loans	1.9	0.7	1.2	2.9	1.1	1.8
Other loans	1.8	0.6	1.1	1.4	0.7	1.0

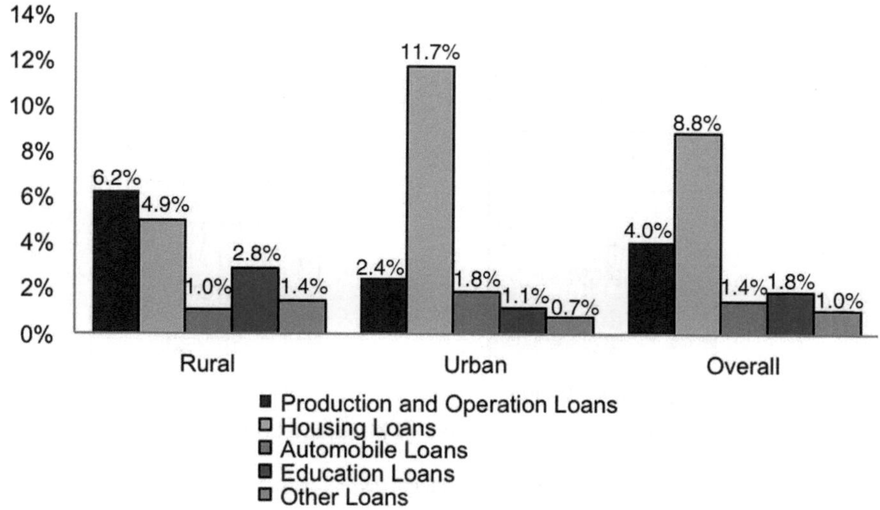

Chart 6.3 Proportion of all loans of households based on rural and urban area in 2013

urban and overall households. This suggests that soaring house prices are imposing great pressure on urban households to have housing loans. The proportion of rural households with automobile loans is also much lower than urban and overall households. This indicates the slow development of automobile consumption credit in the rural areas.

In terms of the proportion of all households' loans, in 2013 rural households carried loans primarily for production and operation activities. 6.2 % of rural households carried such loans; housing loans came the second, accounting for 4.9 %; and education loans came in last, accounting for 2.9 %. For overall households, loans are used in purchasing houses and 8.8 % of households carry such loans. Production and operation activities come in second, accounting for 4 %.

6.2.1.3 Households' Mortgage Loans

In accordance with the loan guarantee, loans can be divided into four categories: credit loans; guaranteed loans; mortgage loans; and pledged loans. The following section analyzes the guaranteed production and operation loans of households in 2013. The production and operation loans can be divided based on industry types into agricultural and business loans.

For agricultural loans, credit loans comprise the highest portion, accounting for approximately 60 %, and are followed by guaranteed loans and mortgage loans, accounting for about 20 %. Pledged loans are the smallest group and account for 1.1 %. The case is different for business loans. The proportion of credit loans also ranks the highest, accounting for approximately 47.2 %, but is still lower than

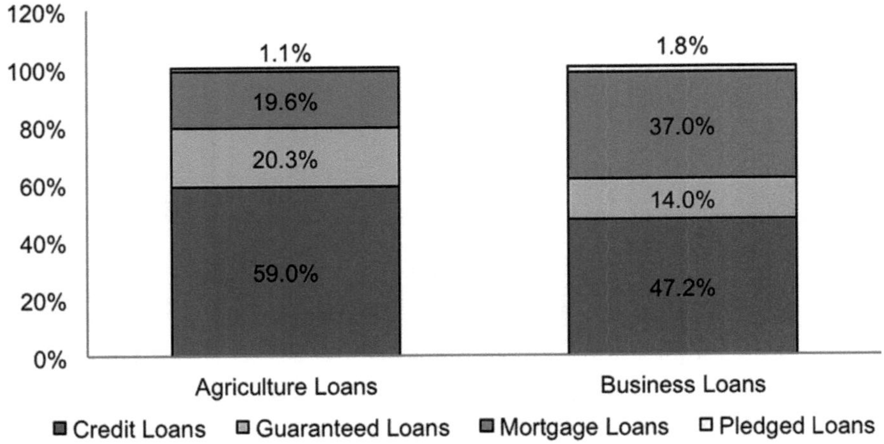

Chart 6.4 Loans on mortgage of households categorized by industries in 2013

agricultural loans. Mortgage loans rank second and account for 37 %. This is followed by guaranteed loans, accounting for 14 %, and pledged loans which are the lowest and account for 1.8 %. See Chart 6.4.

6.2.2 *Private Lending Market*

Chart 6.5 shows the proportion of households with private lending. Compared with 2011, in 2013 the proportion of rural households participating in private lending

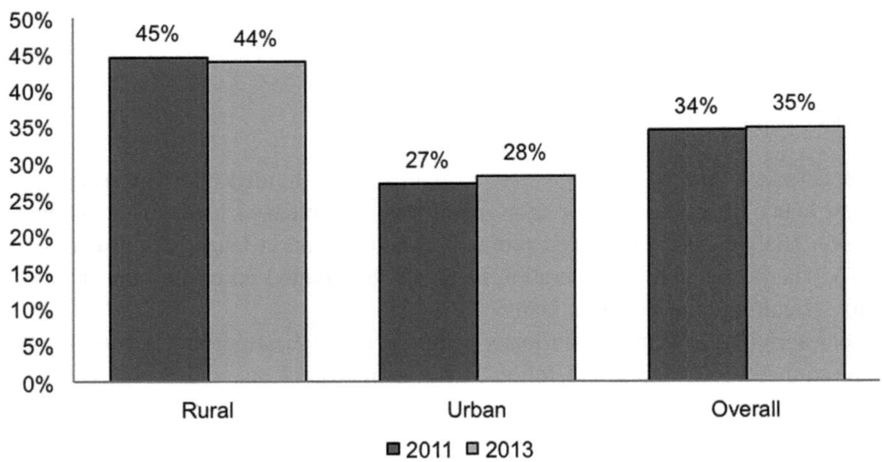

Chart 6.5 General situation of households involved in lending market in 2013

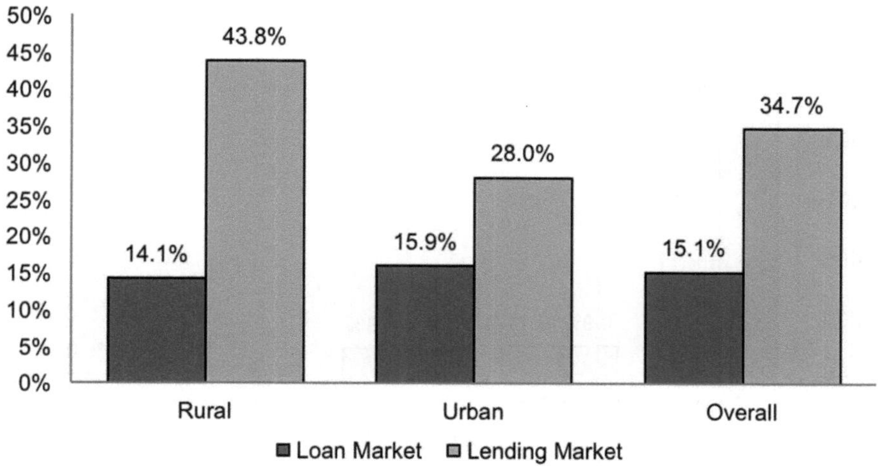

Chart 6.6 Comparison of households involved in loans market and lending market in 2013

fell. There is a significantly higher proportion of rural households with lending than urban households. In 2013, 48.3 % of rural households participated in private lending. This means that almost half of rural households overcome financial shortfalls through private lending.

Chart 6.6 compares household participation in private and formal lending. Regardless of the area, the proportion of households carrying private loans is obviously higher than those with formal loans. This is particularly prominent in rural households, 43.8 % of which carry private loans but only 14.1 % rural households have formal loans. This suggests that rural households overcome financial shortfalls mainly through private lending.

6.3 Finance and Household Consumption

6.3.1 Payment of Household Consumption

6.3.1.1 Comparison of Different Payments

With modern technology becoming increasingly integrated into finance, the payment methods for daily consumption is also changing considerably. In addition to the traditional payment methods of cash and debit card (deposit card), new payment methods, including the semi-credit card, credit card, and shopping card (coupon), are also developing rapidly. As shown in Chart 6.7, from an annual perspective, the methods of payment for households' daily consumption have remained largely unchanged and households' payment habits are largely stable. Comparing payment methods, the prime choice is cash. Data from 2013 shows that 97.3 % households

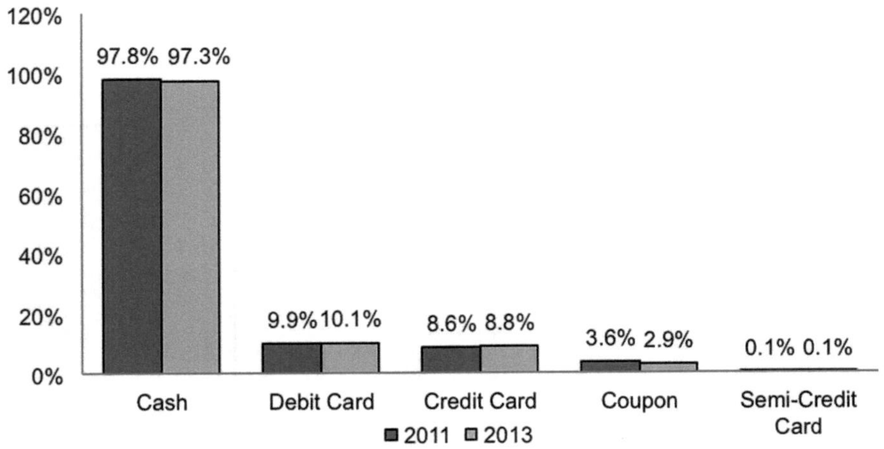

Chart 6.7 Comparison of different payment methods for household consumption

use cash for payment: 10.1 % of them use debit cards; and only 8.8 % of households use credit cards. This shows that modern payment methods are not common in the rural areas and that there is considerable room for development.

6.3.1.2 Non-cash Payment for Household Consumption

The method of payment is classifieds into cash and non-cash payment. Chart 6.8 shows the non-cash payment for household consumption. Annually, the amount of

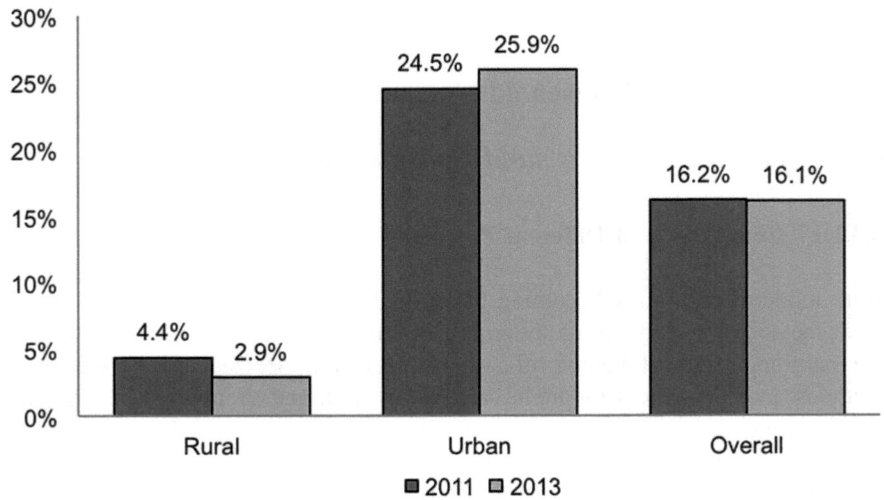

Chart 6.8 Proportion of non-cash payment of household consumption

non-cash payment for household consumption has remained unchanged. From a rural and urban area perspective, non-cash payment in rural households is less popular than in urban areas. The proportion is also below the overall level. Take the 2013 data as an example. Non-cash payment accounts for only 2.9 % of rural household consumption while it is 16.1 % for overall household consumption.

6.3.2 Credit Card Payment for Household Consumption

As an electronic and modern financial means of consumption, the credit card is universally used in Europe and developed western countries, but it is still in its infancy in China. Compare the results of the two years, regardless of the areas; the proportion of households using credit cards for payment is basically unchanged. Comparing the disparity between the rural and urban areas, we can find that the proportion of rural households with credit cards is significantly lower than overall and urban households. The 2013 data shows that only 2.1 % of rural households have credit cards and 5.1 % of overall household do. Generally, credit cards are not very popular with Chinese households and most of households view debt negatively. The potential of the credit card market needs to be further developed. See Chart 6.9.

A later section will further analyze the number of credit cards that households possess. As shown in Chart 6.10, 1.37 % of rural households have credit cards, lower than 1.37 and 1.39 % of overall and urban households, respectively.

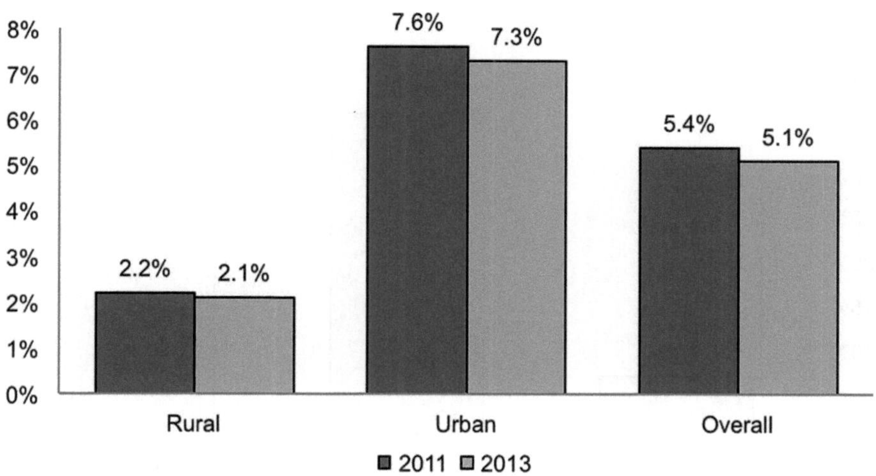

Chart 6.9 Proportion of credit card used in household consumption

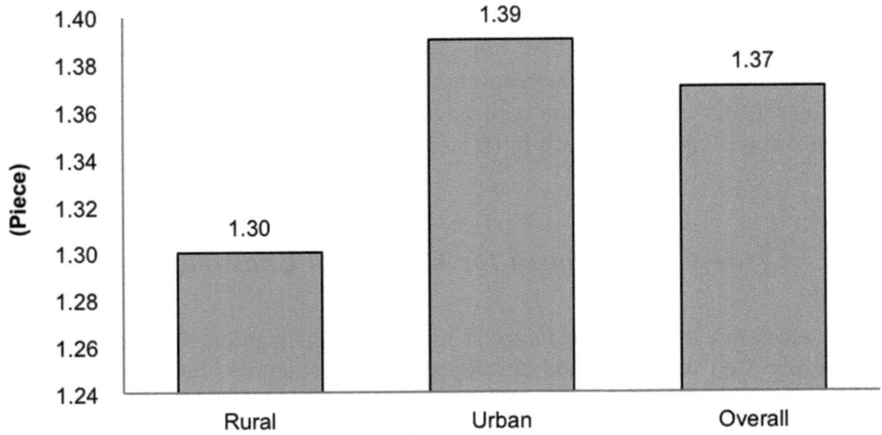

Chart 6.10 Quantity of credit card of household in 2013

6.3.3 Household Online Shopping

6.3.3.1 Participation of Households in Online Shopping

As shown in Chart 6.11, from the urban-rural perspective, 7.1 % of rural households shop online while 24.0 % of all households and 36.5 % of urban households do. The data suggests that this newly developing shopping method prevails in urban areas but lags behind in rural areas. This is a direct result of the rural areas' low levels of education and internet coverage.

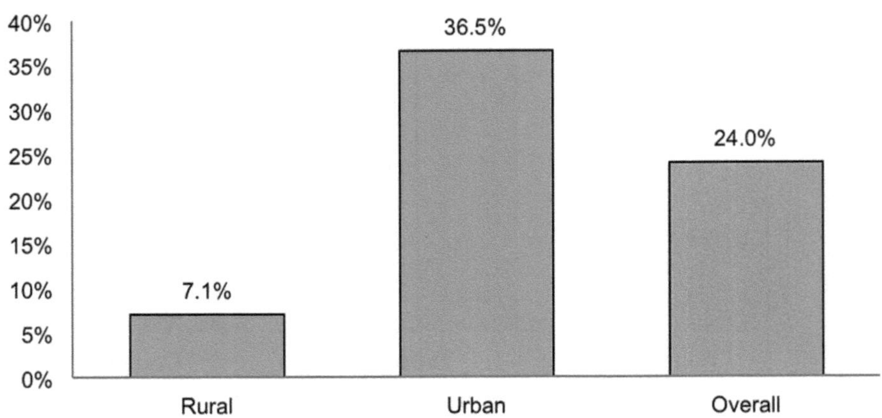

Chart 6.11 Proportion of online shopping of household in 2013

Table 6.3 Selection of household on online shopping payment in 2013 (*unit %*)

	Internet bank	Alipay	Pay on delivery	Payment from others	Credit card	Tenpay
Rural	41.8	32.2	13.9	10.7	1.1	0.3
Urban	33.3	45.2	9.5	5.7	5.9	0.4
Overall	34.3	43.7	10.0	6.2	5.5	0.3

6.3.3.2 Selection of Online Shopping Payment

Table 6.3 shows how households pay for online shopping. 41.8 % of rural households choose to pay with internet banking. This is followed by Alipay (32.2 %) and paying on delivery (13.9 %). For urban and overall households, the highest amount uses Alipay with internet banking and payment on delivery comes in second.

6.3.3.3 Distribution of Internet Banking

Table 6.4 illustrates that the Industrial and Commercial Bank of China (ICBC), Agricultural Bank of China (ABC), and China Construction Bank (CCB) are frequently chosen by households to pay for online shopping. The three state-owned banks have dominant positions in the online banking market. For rural households, ICBC is the most popular choice for paying online, accounting for 29.1 % of households. ABC comes in second and accounts for 28.3 %. This shows the significant role that state-owned banks have played in supporting agriculture and benefiting farmers. CCB came in third, accounting for 23.5 %. The proportion of households choosing the aforementioned three banks exceeds 80 %, suggesting a highly concentrated rural internet banking market. The proportion of rural households that choose Postal Savings Bank of China (PSBC) and Rural Credit Cooperatives (RCC) for payment are 8.4 and 3.9 %, respectively. The two banks also play leading roles as rural financial institutions. For overall households, the

Table 6.4 Distribution of household's selection of internet bank on online shopping in 2013 (*unit %*)

Name of bank	Rural	Urban	Overall
ICBC	29.1	26.7	26.9
ABC	28.3	13.0	14.7
CCB	23.5	24.2	24.1
PSBC	8.4	4.5	5.0
RCC	3.9	0.9	1.2
BOC	2.9	7.5	7.0
CMB	1.2	9.9	8.9
BC	0.5	4.0	3.6
Other banks	2.2	9.3	8.6

proportion choosing ICBC, CCB, and ABC for payment are 26.9, 24.1, and 14.7 %, respectively, ranking as the top three in the internet banking market and jointly exceeding 60 %. They are followed by China Merchants Bank (CMB) and Bank of China (BOC), accounting for 8.9 and 7.0 %, respectively. This shows that in nationwide joint-stock commercial banks, CMB's online banking is better developed. Generally speaking, there is incomplete competition in the internet banking market, especially in the rural areas. The market is over-centralized and needs to be developed as a healthy financial market with reasonable competition and vitality. We should also strive to develop rural finance.

6.4 Household Financial Services and Selection of Bank of Deposit

6.4.1 Financial Services

CHFS (2013) surveyed the number of bank outlets at the village (community) level to measure these places' financial service development. As shown in Chart 6.12, each village had an average of 0.7 bank outlets in the rural areas and 2.63 in the urban areas. Therefore, there is a significant disparity in the financial services' development between the rural and urban areas.

Table 6.5 shows the bank outlets in villages (communities). As shown in Table 6.5, 61.8 % of villages in rural areas have no bank outlets, far higher than the 24.1 % in urban areas. Judging from the number of bank outlets in villages (communities), the proportion of rural areas possessing two or more bank outlets is also far less than the urban areas.

Chart 6.13 shows the average number of banks in the eastern, central, and western rural areas. Judging from Chart 6.13, the number of banks in villages in the

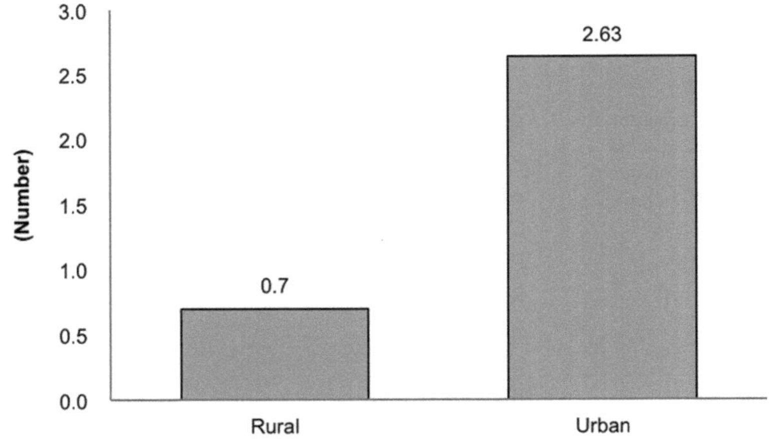

Chart 6.12 Comparison of bank outlets in rural and urban area

Table 6.5 Distribution of number of bank outlet in village (community)

	0	1	2	3	4	5 and above
Rural (%)	61.8	20.4	10.7	4.7	1.3	1.2
Urban (%)	24.1	16.9	17.1	17.5	7.2	12.1

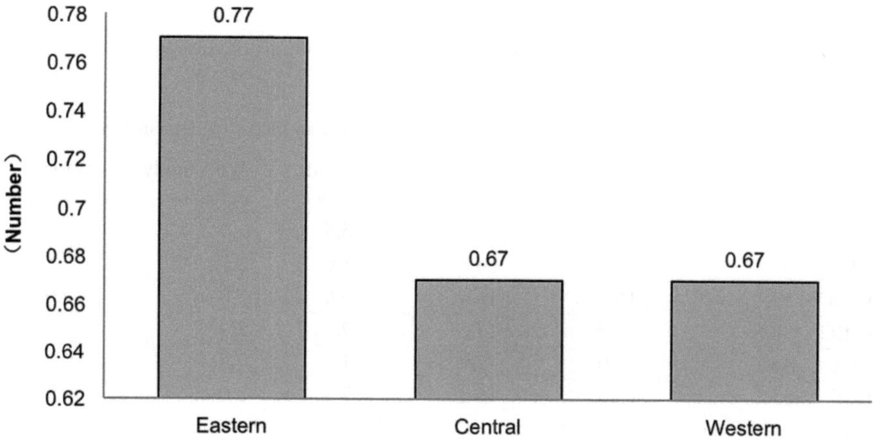

Chart 6.13 Regional disparity of banks in village

eastern region is 0.77, higher than the central and western regions. This means that the number of rural financial services in the eastern region is higher than in the central and western regions.

6.4.2 *Households' Reasons for Choosing Banks of Deposit*

Table 6.6 shows the distribution of households' choices for banks of deposit. As Table 6.6 shows, in rural areas, the top three household banks of deposit are RCC, ABC, and PSBC, respectively. In urban areas, they are ICBC, ABC, and CCB.

Table 6.6 Distribution of household bank of deposits in urban and rural areas (*unit %*)

Distribution of household bank of deposit in urban area		Distribution of household bank of deposit in rural area	
ICBC	23.4	RCC	44.2
ABC	18.1	ABC	22.1
CCB	15.8	PSBC	18.2
PSBC	10.9	ICBC	4.8
RCC	9.2	CCB	3.4
BOC	6.5	BOC	1.3
Other banks	16.1	Other banks	6.0

Table 6.7 Reasons for choosing bank of deposits of households (*unit* %)

	Convenient location	Pay card/pension	Convenient time	Sound service	Work/study demands	More ATM
Overall	47.4	36.8	11.2	7.2	5.1	4.9
Urban	42.5	44.7	8.4	7.0	5.8	5.4
Rural	58.3	19.2	17.4	7.5	3.5	3.6

Note Multiple choices were provided and the table only lists the major reasons

Table 6.8 Rural households' reasons for choosing all banks as banks of deposit (*unit* %)

	Convenient location	Pay card/pension	Convenient time	Sound service	Work/study demands	More ATM
RCC	59.5	17.8	18.5	6.5	2.3	1.5
ABC	57.4	14.4	14.8	8.6	2.7	5.5
PSBC	59.4	16.1	16.6	6.6	3.0	2.9
ICBC	38.6	28.7	11.2	7.9	8.2	12.9
CCB	46.1	27.0	9.9	11.0	7.3	6.2
BOC	33.2	29.6	15.0	7.3	5.6	4.9

Note Multiple choices were provided and the table only lists the major reasons

Table 6.7 analyzes the reasons that households choose banks of deposit. Judging from Table 6.7, the most important reason for choosing a bank of deposit is convenient location, the second is whether bank pays out relevant benefits (including pensions and direct deposits), the third is convenient time and good service.

Table 6.8 shows rural households' reasons for choosing all banks as banks of deposit. Judging from Table 6.8, so many are choosing RCC, ABC, and PSBC because their locations are much more convenient than other banks. This means that the main reason for rural households choosing a bank of deposit is its convenient location.

Chapter 7
Rural Households' Formal Credit Demand and Availability

Overall, the formal credit demand of households is 18.4 % and the availability is 40.5 %. The formal credit demand of rural households is 19.6 % and the availability is 27.6 %. From the usage perspective, rural households' formal credit demand for agricultural production is 24.4 % and the credit availability is 31.3 %; this is far below the industrial and commercial formal credit availability of 44.8 %. According to the regulations for the integrated construction land market established by the government, if rural households can get bank mortgages for agricultural land or homesteads to improve repayment security, then the loan application's probability of being approved increases by approximately 20 %. A small proportion of banks reject loans application on the basis that no collateral is provided, however, and it imposes a small influence on household credit availability. Overall, formal credit availability and formal credit volume decrease as household income decreases. However, the financial system's inclusiveness prevents the formal credit availability of low-income households from decreasing anymore and even causes it to present a carryover effect.

7.1 Formal Credit Demand

7.1.1 Definition of Formal Credit Demand

The formal credit demand of rural household refers to the loan demand towards formal credit institutions for economic activities like production and operation, house and vehicle purchases, and daily consumption. It includes actual and potential formal credit demand. Actual formal credit demand means that households submit the application to formal credit institutions. Potential formal credit demand means that household has credit demand, but no loan demand is proposed to the institutions. In this report, according to CHFS' relative regulations, households with

L. Gan et al., *Report on the Development of Household Finance in Rural China (2014)*, DOI 10.1007/978-981-10-0409-4_7

Table 7.1 Formal credit total demand (*unit %*)

	Overall	Rural
Formal credit total demand	18.4	19.6

formal credit demand can be divided into the following two categories: first, households obtaining bank loans; and second, households fail to obtain bank loans due to "having a loan demand but not submitting an application" and "application submitted but rejected".[1]

Formal credit demand results from agricultural production, business operations, house and vehicle purchases, daily consumption, etc. Therefore, in this chapter, we will first analyze the present condition of households' total credit demands and compare the disparity of total credit demands between overall and rural area. Secondly, we make further discuss and compare different credit purposes. Finally, we comprehensively summarize all the factors imposed on household credit demand.

7.1.2 Analysis of Formal Credit Demand

7.1.2.1 Analysis of Total Formal Credit Demand

According to the statistics of CHFS 2013, 18.4 % of all households have a formal credit demand. In the rural areas, 19.6 % of households have a formal credit demand see Table 7.1. Here, formal credit demand has all kinds of loans purposes, including agricultural production, business operation, house and vehicle purchase, daily consumption, etc. We find that formal credit demand of rural households is not less than all households. The rural area's economic development lags behind the urban areas and the income of rural households is relatively low. Therefore, rural households have a strong interest in applying for loans for production, operation, investment, and consumption.

7.1.2.2 Analysis of Agricultural Production Credit Demand

Of the households engaged in agricultural production, 24.4 % have a credit demand for agricultural production. See Table 7.2. This suggests that rural households have a large demand for agricultural production loans.

[1]If households fail to obtain loans due to "having a demand for loans but not submitting an application" or "application submitted but was rejected," we will refer to this as "credit constraint." This means that the household has credit demand, but fails to obtain loans for its own or other reasons. Another kind of credit constraint refers to actually obtaining loans but in an amount that is less than the amount applied for or demanded. See related essays in Ke Chen Chen and Mali Chivakul (2008), Jappeli (1990), Crook (2001), and Benito and Mumtax (2006).

Table 7.2 Agriculture production credit demand (*unit* %)

	Rural
Agriculture production credit demand	24.4

Table 7.3 Business operation credit demand (*unit* %)

	Overall	Rural
Business operation credit demand	22.0	30.4

7.1.2.3 Analysis of Business Operation Credit Demand

Of the households engaged in business operation, 22.0 % of all households and 30.4 % of rural households have a credit demand for business operation. See Table 7.3. The proportion of rural households with a business operation credit demand is significantly higher than the overall level. Rural households which are engaged in business operation activities that are self-employed or have small and micro businesses demand a smaller amount of funds, but the proportion of demand is relatively high. The data shows that rural households have a strong demand for business operation loans.

7.1.2.4 Analysis of Housing Credit Demand

Among households that have purchased or constructed houses, 20.7 % of all households and 23.7 % of rural households have a housing credit demand. See Table 7.4. The rural area's proportion of housing credit demand is higher than that of overall households. Although the proportion of rural households purchasing commodity houses is low and most rural households construct houses by themselves, rural households still have a great demand for housing credit loans.

7.1.2.5 Analysis of Automobile Credit Demand

Among households that have purchased automobiles, 13.6 % of all households and 21.4 % of rural households have an automobile credit demand. See Table 7.5. The

Table 7.4 Housing credit demand (*unit* %)

	Overall	Rural
Housing credit demand	20.7	23.7

Table 7.5 Automobile credit demand (*unit* %)

	Overall	Rural
Automobile credit demand	13.6	21.4

Table 7.6 Credit card demand (*unit* %)

	Overall	Rural
Credit card demand	15.9	11.8

proportion of rural households with an automobile credit demand is significantly higher than that of overall households. Although the proportion of rural households purchasing automobiles is lower than that of urban households, rural households have a greater demand for automobile credit loans (if they decide to purchase automobiles).

7.1.2.6 Analysis of Credit Card Demand

According to CHFS' statistics, 15.9 % of all households and 11.8 % of rural households have a credit card demand. See Table 7.6. Rural households' proportion of credit card demand is significantly lower than that of overall households. As rural households are not familiar with credit cards and they prefer cash payments, there is a small demand for credit cards.

7.1.3 Factor Analysis of Formal Credit Demand

7.1.3.1 Factor Analysis of Agricultural Production Credit Demand

As the survey shows, using the rural areas as an example, agricultural production credit demand is contributed to by factors including household income and demographics.

First, we analyze the relationship between agricultural production credit demand and income. We divide household income into six groups from low income to high. See Table 7.7 for details. The data shows that low-income households have the strongest demand for agricultural production credit loans. The result also happens in the eastern, central, and western regions; the agricultural production credit demand

Table 7.7 Household income and agricultural production credit demand (*unit* Yuan)

Rural	Proportion of credit demand (%)
Annual household income below 10,000 (not included)	26.9
Annual household income of 10,000–40,000 (not included)	25.0
Annual household income of 40,000–80,000 (not included)	20.6
Annual household income of 80,000–150,000 (not included)	22.1
Annual household income of 150,000–1,000,000 (not included)	21.9
Annual household income above 1,000,000	9.8

Table 7.8 Regional distribution and agricultural production credit demand (*unit* %)

Rural	Proportion of credit demand (%)
Eastern	17.6
Central	24.7
Western	29.2

Table 7.9 Agricultural subsidies and agricultural production credit demand (*unit* %)

Rural	Proportion of credit demand (%)
Households with agricultural subsidies	23.6
Households without agricultural subsidies	27.6

successively increases from east to west as the level of economic development decreases. This also suggests that the less developed the area is, the stronger the agricultural production credit demand is. See Table 7.8 for specific results. Agricultural subsidies increase rural households' incomes, in turn significantly reducing the agricultural production credit demand. See Table 7.9 for relative results. This illustrates that in households engaged in agricultural production, income is one of the important factors influencing agricultural production credit demand. Most households engaged in agricultural production live in the rural areas. Because the rural households are poorer and less developed, more rural households depend on agricultural production. Therefore, low-income rural households have a strong demand for agricultural production credit. A credit policy that favors low-income-households is necessary. This survey result provides a realistic basis for the necessity of implementing inclusive financial policies.

Second, we analyze the relationship between agricultural production credit demand and demographic characteristics. We divide the age of the head of household into six groups from youngest to oldest. (See Table 7.10 for details.) The data shows that agricultural production credit demand is mainly embodied in young and middle-aged households. This result is consistent with the findings of foreign scholars. According to the life cycle theory, we make age grouping statistics and the age distribution's household credit demand presents an inverted-U-shaped structure. The result of analyzing household size and agricultural production credit

Table 7.10 Age of head of household and agricultural production credit demand

Rural	Proportion of credit demand (%)
Age of head of household: 16–25 years old (not included)	23.8
Age of head of household: 25–35 years old (not included)	29.6
Age of head of household: 35–45 years old (not included)	29.2
Age of head of household: 45–55 years old (not included)	28.0
Age of head of household: 55–65 years old (not included)	21.4
Age of head of household above 65 years old	15.0

Table 7.11 Household size and agriculture production credit demand

Rural	Proportion of credit demand (%)
Household size: 1 person	16.8
Household size: 2 people	18.2
Household size: 3–4 people (included)	25.8
Household size: 5–6 people(included)	26.0
Household size: more than 6 people	27.0

demand shows that the more household members there are, the stronger the agricultural production credit demand is. See Table 7.11 for details.

7.1.3.2 Factor Analysis of Business Operation Credit Demand

As the survey results show, there are several factors that contribute to business operation credit demand, including household income and subjective attitudes.

First, we analyze the relationship between the business operation credit demand and household income. We also divided household income into six groups from low to high. See Table 7.12 for detailed grouping standards. The data shows that income has an impact on business operation credit demand, both overall and in rural areas, presenting an obvious U-shaped structure. Households with the lowest incomes and highest incomes have strong demands for business operation credit. (See Tables 7.12, 7.13, and Chart 7.1.)

Second, we analyze the relationship between business operation credit demand and subjective attitudes. From the perspective of the attitudes towards risk, the demand for business operation credit of households with risk preference is significantly higher than that of risk averse households. (See Table 7.14 for details.) Households' attention to financial information also significantly influences business operation credit demand. Analysis of Table 7.15 illustrates that rural households that pay extremely high attention to economic and financial information have twice as much as demand for business operation credit as rural households that pay no

Table 7.12 Household income and business operation credit demand (overall) (*unit* Yuan)

Overall	Proportion of credit demand (%)
Annual household income below 10,000 (not included)	39.8
Annual household income of 10,000–40,000 (not included)	26.7
Annual household income of 40,000–80,000 (not included)	22.2
Annual household income of 80,000–150,000 (not included)	16.5
Annual household income of 150,000–1,000,000 (not included)	28.3
Annual household income above 1,000,000	35.5

Table 7.13 Household income and business operation credit demand (rural) (*unit* Yuan)

Rural	Proportion of credit demand (%)
Annual household income below 10,000 Yuan (not included)	39.1
Annual household income of 10,000–40,000 (not included)	30.7
Annual household income of 40,000–80,000 (not included)	27.9
Annual household income of 80,000–150,000 (not included)	22.5
Annual household income of 150,000–1,000,000 (not included)	36.7
Annual household income above 1,000,000	51.0

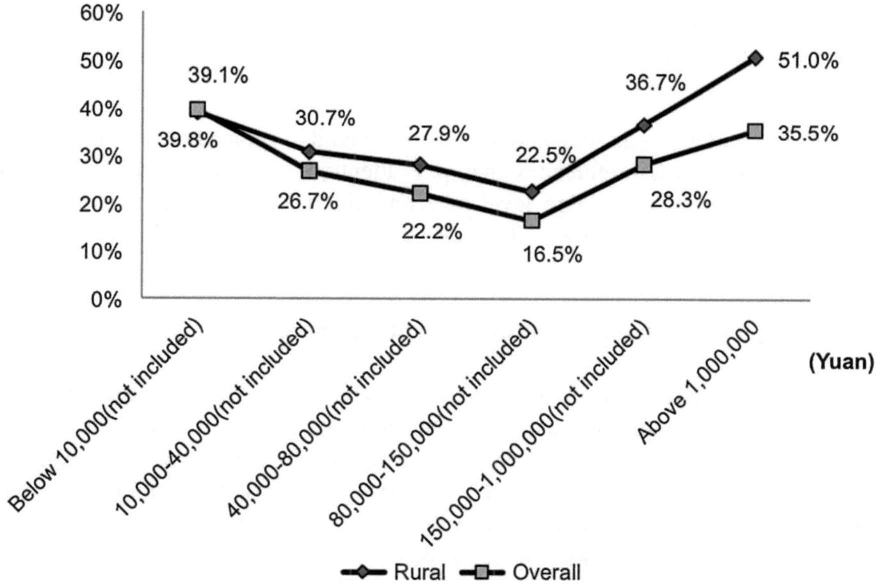

Chart 7.1 Household income and business operation credit demand

Table 7.14 Risk attitude and business operation credit demand

Overall	Proportion of credit demand (%)
Extreme risk preference	34.0
Risk preference	27.6
Risk neutral	28.3
Risk aversion	24.4
Extreme risk aversion	22.3

attention to economic and financial information. In addition, rural households with economic or financial training also have higher business operation credit demands. (See Table 7.16 for details.) Above all, there is a close relationship between

Table 7.15 Attention to economic and financial information and business operation credit demand

Rural	Proportion of credit demand (%)
Extremely high attention	58.1
High attention	43.7
Ordinary attention	29.7
Low attention	24.9
No attention	27.3

Table 7.16 Economic and financial knowledge level and business operation credit demand

Rural	Proportion of credit demand (%)
Households with economic or financial training	37.7
Households without economic or financial training	30.0

business operation credit demand and a household's subjective attitude. Rural households with risk preferences that pay attention to economic and financial information and possess a high level of economic and financial knowledge have stronger demands for business and operation credit.

7.1.3.3 Factor Analysis of Housing Credit Demand

As the survey results show, housing credit demand is closely related to household income level. We divide household income into six groups from low income to high. (See Table 7.17 for details.) The data shows that the housing credit demand of high-income households is obviously smaller than that of lower-middle-income households. The result also happens in the eastern, central, and western regions. Table 7.18 shows that the housing credit demand successively increases from east to west as economic development decreases. This also suggests that the less developed an area is, the stronger its housing credit demand is. Household size is

Table 7.17 Household income and housing credit demand (*unit* Yuan)

Rural	Proportion of credit demand (%)
Annual household income below 10,000 Yuan (not included)	24.5
Annual household income of 10,000–40,000 (not included)	24.0
Annual household income of 40,000–80,000 (not included)	23.3
Annual household income of 80,000–150,000 (not included)	24.2
Annual household income of 150,000–1,000,000 (not included)	15.8
Annual household income of more than 1,000,000	13.7

Table 7.18 Regional distribution and housing credit demand (*unit %*)

Rural	Proportion of credit demand (%)
Eastern	19.6
Central	24.1
Western	27.2

Table 7.19 Household size and housing credit demand

Rural	Proportion of credit demand (%)
Household size: 1 person	14.1
Household size: 2 people	16.4
Household size: 3–4 people (included)	25.1
Household size: 5–6 people (included)	27.1
Household size: more than 6 people	26.6

another factor that influences housing credit demand. Households with several people have a significantly higher housing credit demand than households with one or two people.

See Table 7.19 for specific results.

7.1.3.4 Factor Analysis of Credit Card Demand

As the survey results show, several factors contribute to credit card demand, including level of financial knowledge and subjective attitude.

We use the head of household's educational background to show the relationship between credit demand and level of education. The more education he or she has, the greater his or her demand for credit is. Chart 7.2 shows that for overall and rural households, the more education a head of household receives, the stronger his or her demand for credit cards is. Similarly, in Table 7.20 we find that the credit card demand of households with economic or financial training is significantly higher than that of households without training. Households' attention to financial information also relates to credit card demand; the more attention they pay, the stronger their demand for credit cards is. See Chart 7.3 for detailed results.

We also find that credit card demand is closely related to attitude towards risk. The credit card demand of households with risk preference is significantly higher than that of risk averse households. See Table 7.21 for specific results. The influence of income on credit card demand presents different characteristics than other kinds of credit demand. The higher the household's income, the stronger its demand for a credit card is. See Table 7.22 for specific results. In conclusion, as a newly developed credit form, the credit card is commonly accepted by people with high incomes, high levels of education, and certain economic and financial knowledge.

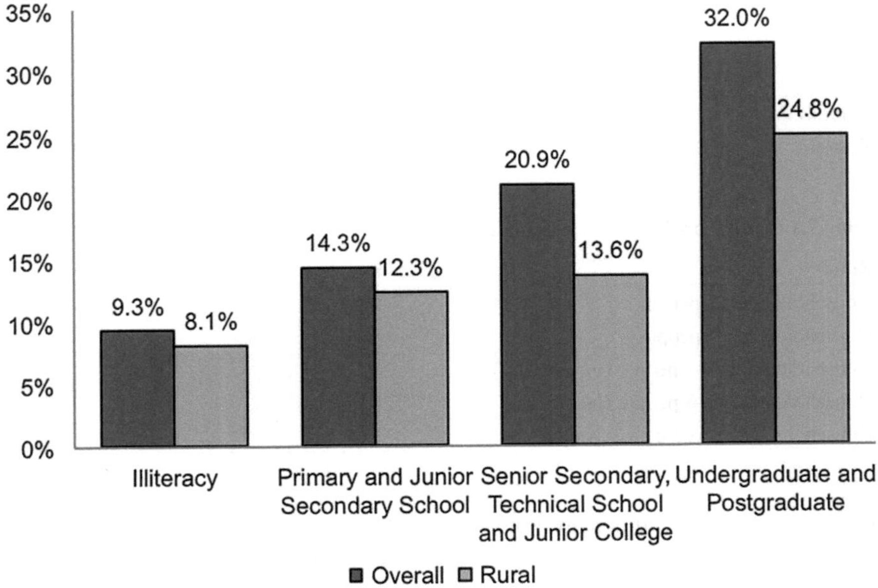

Chart 7.2 Education and credit card demand

Table 7.20 Economic and financial knowledge and credit card demand

Rural	Proportion of credit demand (%)
Households with economic or financial training	14.5
Households without economic or financial training	11.7

7.2 Formal Credit Availability

7.2.1 Construction of Formal Credit Availability Index

The formal credit availability index measures how formal credit is available. It generally refers to the proportion of households that received actual loans and households that have formal credit demand with values ranging from 0 to 1. For example, if the formal credit index is 60 %, it means that out of 100 households with a formal credit demand, 60 of them can receive actual bank loans.

Specifically, the formal credit index is constructed as follows:

$$\text{Formal Credit Index} = \frac{\text{Number of Households Receiving Loans}}{\text{Number of Households Holding Formal Credit Demand}}$$

Formal Credit Index = Number of Households Receiving Loans/Number of Households Holding Formal Credit Demand

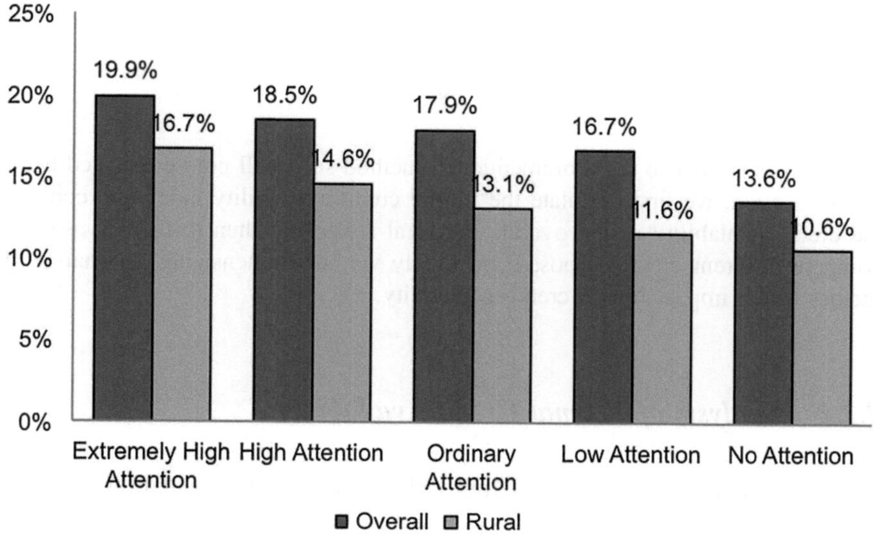

Chart 7.3 Attention to economic and financial information and credit card demand

Table 7.21 Risk attitude and credit card demand

Overall	Proportion of credit demand (%)
Extreme risk preference	16.4
Risk preference	15.5
Risk neutral	15.3
Risk aversion	11.9
Extreme risk aversion	1.1

Table 7.22 Household income and credit card demand (*unit* Yuan)

Overall	Proportion of credit demand (%)
Annual household income below 10,000 (not included)	14.8
Annual household income of 10,000–40,000 (not included)	15.6
Annual household income of 40,000–80,000 (not included)	15.1
Annual household income of 80,000–150,000 (not included)	17.0
Annual household income of 150,000–1,000,000 (not included)	25.1
Annual household income above 1,000,000	51.1

Due to different purposes, the formal credit availability index can be divided into the agricultural production credit availability index, the business operation credit availability index, the housing credit availability index, the automobile credit availability index, and the credit card availability index. (The construction of all the

Table 7.23 General index of formal credit availability (*unit* %)

	Overall	Rural
Formal credit availability	40.5	27.6

sub-items is similar to the aforementioned method so it will not be repeated here.) In this section, we first calculate the formal credit availability index and compare the credit availability of the overall and rural areas. We then further discuss and compare different credit purposes and finally we comprehensively summarize all factors which impact formal credit availability.

7.2.2 *Analysis of Formal Credit Availability*

7.2.2.1 Analysis of the General Index of Formal Credit Availability

Over the past 20 years, all domestic and overseas theoretical research and experience analysis has shown that rural households in developing countries are financially repressed as a result of an incomplete market. Examples include the interest rate cap set by government, monopoly in informal credit market, moral hazard, etc. The CHFS results show that the formal credit availability of overall households is 40.5 and 27.6 % for rural households. (See Table 7.23.) The credit availability of rural households is far less than for overall households. This shows that like many other developing countries, China's rural households are also being severely financially repressed.

Further analysis of financial repression shows that in households with credit demand, 59.5 % of all households are constrained by credit and 53.5 % of these households have credit demands but have not submitted an application to the bank. 6.0 % of households have applied for bank loans but been rejected. Financial repression is more severe in the rural areas; 72.4 % of rural households are constrained by credit, 62.7 % of these households have credit demands but have not submitted an application to the bank, and 9.7 % of households applied for loans but have been rejected by the bank (Table 7.24).

Table 7.24 Proportion of credit constraints (*unit* %)

	Overall	Rural
Proportion of credit constraint	59.5	72.4
– Proportion of no application submitted	53.5	62.7
– Proportion of applications submitted but rejected	6.0	9.7

Table 7.25 Agriculture production credit availability (*unit* %)

	Rural
Agricultural production credit availability	31.3

Table 7.26 Business operation credit availability (*unit* %)

	Overall	Rural
Business operation credit availability	47.6	44.8

7.2.2.2 Analysis of Agricultural Production Credit Availability

The survey results show that for households engaged in agricultural production, the agricultural production credit availability is 31.34 %. (See Table 7.25.) The agricultural production credit availability in rural area needs to be further improved.

7.2.2.3 Analysis of Business Operation Credit Availability

The survey results show that for households engaged in business operation, the business operation credit availability of overall households is 47.6 and 44.8 % for rural households. (See Table 7.25.) The business operation credit availability of rural households is lower than that of overall households. On the whole, the business operation credit availability if significantly higher than the agricultural production credit availability (Table 7.26).

7.2.2.4 Analysis of Housing Credit Availability

Table 7.27 shows that for households that have purchased or constructed houses, the housing credit availability of overall households is 51.1 and 25.4 % for rural households. The housing credit availability of rural households is lower than that of overall households. There is a small proportion of rural households purchasing commodity houses and most of them construct houses by themselves. The data shows that rural households are under great financial pressure when purchasing or constructing houses and have severe credit constraints.

Table 7.27 Housing credit availability (*unit* %)

	Overall	Rural
Housing credit availability	51.1	25.4

Table 7.28 Automobile credit availability (*unit* %)

	Overall	Rural
Automobile credit availability	61.1	48.9

Table 7.29 Credit card availability (*unit* %)

	Overall	Rural
Credit card availability	40.5	27.6
Rejection rate of application	3.0	2.2
Not applying despite in need	61.8	79.4

7.2.2.5 Analysis of Automobile Credit Availability

Table 7.28 shows that for households that have purchased automobiles, the automobile credit availability of overall households is 61.1 and 48.9 % for rural households. The automobile credit availability of rural households is lower than overall households. Automobile credit belongs to mortgage loans and its loan fund is generally lower than housing mortgage loans which mature in a short time. Therefore, the availability of automobile credit is higher than others.

7.2.2.6 Analysis of Credit Card Availability

As the survey results show, among all households in need of credit cards, 40.5 % of all households had successful applications while only 27.6 % of rural households did. Table 7.29 shows that the rejection rate for credit card applications is in fact very low and the majority of households, despite needing credit cards, do not apply for them out of repayment concerns, etc.

7.2.3 *Factor Analysis of Formal Credit Availability*

7.2.3.1 Factor Analysis of Agricultural Production Credit Availability

As shown in the survey, several factors affect the availability of agricultural production credit, including education, economic and financial knowledge, and income. Table 7.30 shows that as the head of household receives more education, his or her agricultural production credit availability rises. According to Table 7.31, regardless of if it is in overall or just rural areas, households with members that have attended economic and financial training courses receive significantly higher agricultural production credit availability than those without such training. Chart 7.4 illustrates that households that pay more attention to economic and financial

Table 7.30 Education and agricultural production credit availability (*unit %*)

Overall	Credit availability index
Illiteracy	23.9
Primary and junior secondary school	30.4
Senior secondary, technical school, or junior college	40.3
Undergraduate and postgraduate	62.4

Table 7.31 Knowledge of economics and finance and agricultural production credit availability (*unit %*)

	Overall	Rural
With economic and financial training courses	44.62	48.7
Without economic and financial training courses	30.36	31.0

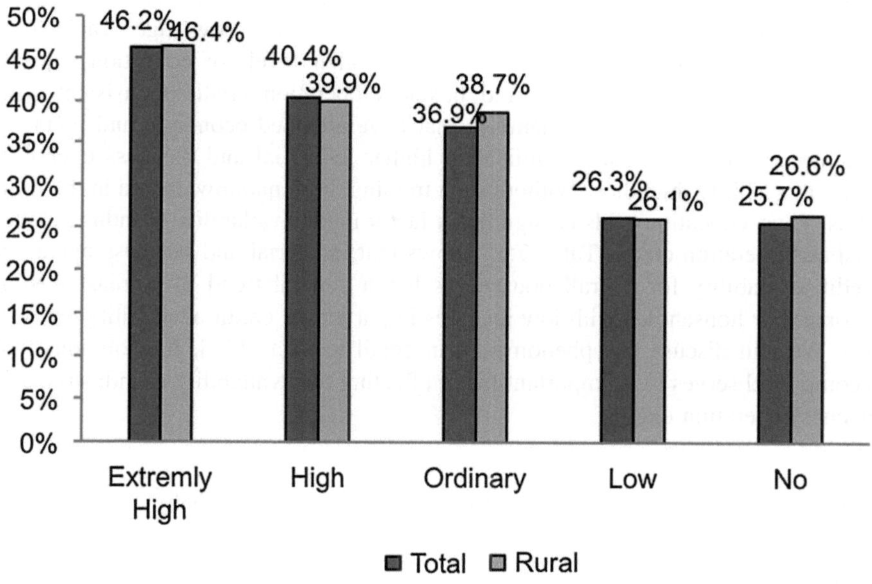

Chart 7.4 Attention to economic and financial information and agricultural production credits

information are more likely to receive agricultural production credit. In conclusion, education has a large impact on agricultural production credit availability.

As shown in Table 7.32, agricultural production credit availability increases as income rises in both the overall and rural areas. Apparently, income level is an important factor affecting the availability of agricultural production credit availability.

Table 7.32 Income and agricultural production credit availability (*unit* Yuan)

	Overall (%)	Rural (%)
Annual household income less than 10,000	24.4	24.9
Annual household income of 10,000–40,000 (not included)	28.1	29.7
Annual household income of 40,000–80,000 (not included)	35.0	37.4
Annual household income of 80,000–150,000 (not included)	53.2	52.4
Annual household income of 150,000–1,000,000 (not included)	59.3	57.2
Annual household income more than 1,000,000	60.9	[a]

[a]Not included since sample size is too small

7.2.3.2 Factor Analysis of Industrial and Business Operation Credit Availability

As shown by the survey's results, similar to agricultural production credit availability, industrial and business operation credit availability is also related to several factors including education and economic and financial knowledge. Table 7.33 shows that households with heads that have higher levels of education enjoy a higher availability of industrial and business operation credit. Consistent with Table 7.34, households with members that have attended economic and financial training courses experience significantly higher industrial and business operation credit availability than those without such training, both nationwide and in the rural areas. Thus, education is also a significant factor in the availability of industrial and business operation credit. Table 7.35 shows that industrial and business operation credit availability for overall households has a general trend of increasing with income. For households with low incomes in particular, credit availability tends to rise. We will discuss this phenomenon in detail in Sect. 7.2.5. It is obvious that income level serves is an important factor affecting the availability of industrial and business operation credits.

Table 7.33 Education and industrial and business operation credit availability

Overall	Credit availability index (%)
Illiteracy	36.3
Primary and junior secondary school	42.5
Senior secondary, technical school, and junior college	53.3
Undergraduate and postgraduate	61.2

Table 7.34 Knowledge of economics and finance and industrial and business operation credit availability (*unit* %)

	Overall	Rural
With economic and financial training courses	61.5	81.9
Without economic and financial training courses	44.8	42.4

Table 7.35 Income and industrial and business operation credit availability (*unit* Yuan)

Overall	Credit availability index (%)
Annual household income less than 10,000	40.2
Annual household income of 10,000 to less than 40,000	34.3
Annual household income of 40,000 to less than 80,000	44.0
Annual household income of 80,000 to less than 150,000	54.2
Annual household income of 150,000 to less than 1,000,000	67.2
Annual household income more than 1,000,000	86.1

7.2.3.3 Factor Analysis of Housing Credit Availability

The survey results show that housing credit availability is related to several factors, including education, income, and demographic characteristics. Table 7.36 shows that households with heads that receive more education enjoy higher housing credit availability. Table 7.37 shows that both in the overall or rural areas, households attending economic and financial training courses all have higher housing credit availability than those without such training. As a consequence, education is also a significant factor in housing credit availability. Table 7.38 shows that housing credit availability for overall households grows in accordance with income increases. As a result, income greatly affects housing credit availability. In the meantime, households in which the heads are young and middle-aged enjoy significantly higher housing credit availability than other age groups. This is because longer lengths for housing loan maturity require certain age restrictions for applicants; thus, young people have the advantage in applying for housing credit. (See Table 7.39 below for detailed results.)

Table 7.36 Education and housing credit availability

Overall	Credit availability index (%)
Illiteracy	21.5
Primary and junior secondary school	32.3
Senior secondary, technical school and junior college	62.7
Undergraduate and postgraduate	85.3

Table 7.37 Knowledge of economics and finance and housing credit availability (*unit* %)

	Overall	Rural
With economic and financial training courses	75.5	37.6
Without economic and financial training courses	42.5	25.2

Table 7.38 Income and housing credit availability (*unit* Yuan)

Overall	Credit availability index (%)
Annual household income less than 10,000	28.4
Annual household income of 10,000–40,000 (not included)	28.6
Annual household income of 40,000–80,000 (not included)	46.8
Annual household income of 80,000–150,000 (not included)	66.5
Annual household income of 150,000–1,000,000 (not included)	87.1
Annual household income more than 1,000,000	93.6

Table 7.39 Ages of head of household and housing credit availability

Overall	Credit availability index (%)
Head of household 16 to less than 25 years old	59.4
Head of household 25 to less than 35 years old	71.4
Head of household 35 to less than 45 years old	52.8
Head of household 45 to less than 55 years old	37.5
Head of household 55 to less than 65 years old	36.3
Head of household over 65 years old	23.8

7.2.3.4 Analysis of Factors Affecting Automobile Credit Availability

As shown by the survey results, automobile credit availability is related to income. Table 7.40 shows that the automobile credit availability for overall households nationwide generally increases as income rises; similar to industrial and business operation credits, automobile credit availability also presents a carryover effect in the lowest income group. Table 7.41 shows that overall automobile credit availability has distinct regional characteristics, declining from the eastern region to the westerns region in accordance with the decreasing level of economic development. In conclusion, income greatly affects automobile credit availability.

Table 7.40 Income and automobile credit availability (*unit* Yuan)

Overall	Credit availability index (%)
Annual household income less than 10,000	43.8
Annual household income of 10,000–40,000 (not included)	40.4
Annual household income of 40,000–80,000 (not included)	53.9
Annual household income of 80,000–150,000 (not included)	63.7
Annual household income of 150,000–1,000,000 (not included)	85.9
Annual household income more than 1,000,000	92.6

Table 7.41 Region and automobile credit availability

Overall	Credit availability index (%)
Eastern	67.0
Central	53.1
Western	52.5

7.2.3.5 Analysis of Factors Affecting Credit Card Availability

As the research results show, credit card availability is related to several factors, including education, economic and financial knowledge, and demographic characteristics. Table 7.42 shows that credit card availability increases significantly as education improves. Table 7.43 also shows that households with certain economic and financial knowledge enjoy higher credit card availability than other households. Regional analysis illustrates that credit card availability increases with regional economic development, and that it successively decreases across the eastern, central, and western regions. See Table 7.44 for details. Meanwhile, credit card availability features obvious age characteristics, meaning that it decreases as the head of household's age increases. (See Table 7.45 for detailed results.)

Table 7.42 Education and credit card availability (*unit* %)

	Overall	Rural
Illiterate	6.7	3.8
Primary and junior secondary school	23.7	18.5
Senior secondary, technical school and junior college	51.1	28.6
Undergraduate and postgraduate	73.4	55.7

Table 7.43 Economic and financial and credit card availability (*unit* %)

	Overall	Rural
With training courses on economics and finance	68.0	30.2
Without training courses on economics and finance	32.3	18.1

Table 7.44 Regional credit card availability (*unit* %)

	Overall	Rural
Eastern	47.8	28.5
Central	28.9	16.9
Western	28.0	13.5

Table 7.45 Ages of head of household and credit card availability

	Overall (%)	Rural (%)
16 to less than 25 years old	24.4	7.2
25 to less than 35 years old	27.2	10.2
35 to less than 45 years old	15.3	6.1
45 to less than 55 years old	9.5	4.2
55 to less than 65 years old	4.9	1.3
Head of household over 65 years old	1.9	0.6

7.2.4 *How Improving the Secondary Market for Rural Land Mortgage Influences on Household Credit Availability*

During the Third Plenary Session of the 18th Communist Party of China (CPC) Central Committee, "The Decision of the CCCPC Regarding Major Issues Concerning Comprehensively Deepening the Reform" was released. According to the public document, the Chinese government will form a unified construction land market for both urban and rural areas in addition to steadily developing and improving the secondary market for land leases, transfers, and mortgages. Improving the secondary market for rural land mortgages is very significant to household credit availability, especially to rural households. Judging from our data, if households with rural land are able to take out a mortgage on their agricultural land or homestead and increase their loan guarantee for repayment, their loan application acceptance rate will increase by about 20 %. Since banks rarely reject applications due to a lack of collateral, however, rural land mortgages in general will have a relatively small impact on household credit availability.

7.2.4.1 Influences on Agricultural Production Credit Availability by Rural Land Mortgage

7.0 % of rural households have agricultural production credit. For those without agricultural production credit, 3.5 % of them have had their credit applications denied. Among the various reasons for refusal, 19.3 % of the applications were rejected due to alack of collateral. Of the rural households lacking collateral, 98.3 % of them possessed land assets, such as agricultural land or homesteads. As a result, as the second market for rural land mortgages is gradually perfected, banks will be able to accept land assets as collateral. The proportion of credits application rejections will decrease by 18.7 % while agricultural production credit availability will increase by 0.70 %.

7.2.4.2 Influences on Industrial and Business Operation Credit Availability by Rural Land Mortgage

13.6 % of rural households possess industrial and business operation credit. For those without industrial and business operation credit, 4.6 % of them had their credit applications rejected. Among the various reasons for refusal, 15.3 % of applications were rejected due to a lack of collateral. Of the rural households lacking collateral, 69.1 % of them possessed land assets such as agricultural land or homesteads. As a result, as the second market for rural land mortgage is gradually perfected, banks will be able to accept land assets as collaterals. The proportion of credit applications that are rejected will decrease by 10.6 % while industrial and business operation credit availability will increase by 0.61 %.

7.2.4.3 Influences on Housing Credit Availability by Rural Land Mortgage

15.3 % of rural households have housing credit. Of those without housing credit, 2.7 % had their credit applications rejected. Of the various reasons for rejection, 20.8 % of applications were rejected due to a lack of collateral. Of the rural households lacking collateral, 100 % of them possessed land assets, such as agricultural land or homesteads. As a result, as the second market for rural land mortgages is gradually perfected, banks will be able to accept land assets as collateral. The proportion of credits application rejections will decrease by 20.8 % while housing credit availability will increase by 0.48 %.

7.2.5 Inclusive Finance and Credit Availability

On November 12, 2013, "The Decision of the CCCPC Regarding Major Issues Concerning Comprehensive Deepening the Reform" was made during the Third Plenary Session of the 18th Communist Party of China (CPC) Central Committee. The government officially states in its decision that "We will develop inclusive finance, encourage financial innovation, and enrich the financial market with more levels and more products." The major reason for inclusive finance is to provide financial services to the large amount of middle and low income people, even in extreme poverty, through financial innovation.

In accordance with the 2013 CHFS (China Household Finance Survey), formal credit availability for overall households is 40.5 %. In other words, if 1000 households need credit, only 406 of them on average will be able to receive credit from the banks. According to the research data, the overall credits demand for households nationwide is 63,000 Yuan per household. Of these, 32,000 Yuan may be obtained through formal credits channels. Formal credit acquisition is also a significant indicator of credit availability. (See Table 7.46.)

Table 7.46 Credits acquisition of different income class (*unit %*)

Income class	Lowest to 10	10–20	20–30	30–40	40–50
Credits demand (Yuan)	76,143	45,221	31,766	42,894	58,841
Formal credits acquisition (Yuan)	21,809	12,827	16,246	11,805	14,042
Income class	50–60	60–70	70–80	80–90	90 to Highest
Credits demand (Yuan)	45,556	41,041	48,467	87,156	202,050
Formal credits acquisition (Yuan)	15,309	23,011	30,479	47,339	170,085

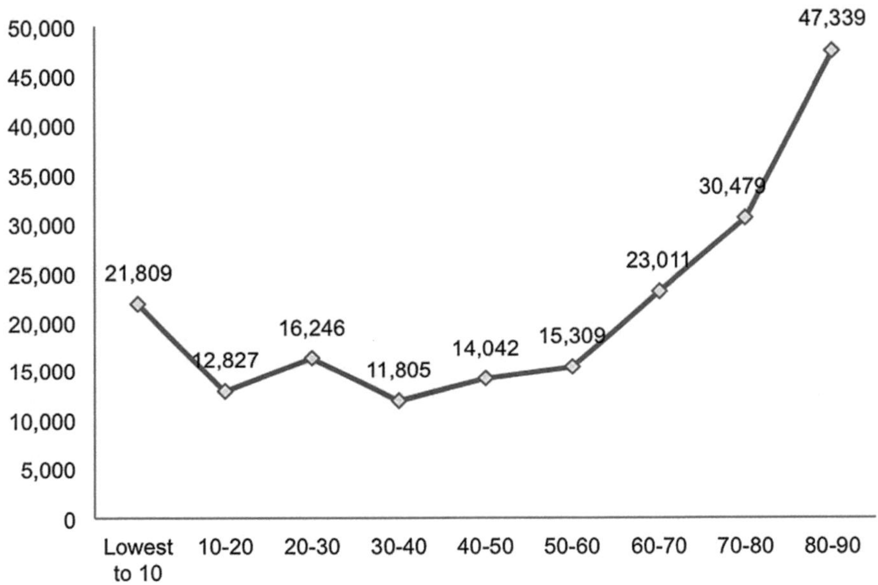

Chart 7.5 Comparison of formal credits acquisition of different income classes

As shown in Chart 7.5, overall households are divided into 10 groups in descending order of income. Since the group with the highest income receives much more formal credit, it has little significance compared to the other groups. Therefore, Chart 7.5 only excludes the highest 10 % of income people. It is clear that formal credit acquisition declines as income decreases in general. For households with low incomes or even in extreme poverty, however, formal credit acquisition picks up significantly. We believe that developing inclusive finance will prevent low-income households from failing to acquire credit. Credit availability even features a carryover effect for such households. By developing inclusive finance, low-income households will face less difficulties when applying for bank loans and receive more actual credit. As inclusive finance expands into a wider range, the carryover effect in credit acquisition for low-income households will become more obvious if the financial strategies which are preferential to households with low incomes or in extreme poverty are well-implemented.

Chapter 8
Financial Risks of Rural Households

This chapter analyzes rural households' financial risks. Data shows that the proportion of indebted rural households is higher than the overall level, but they are have a smaller scale of debts. Rural households in the western region are most indebted yet have the smallest debt scale. Judging from the debt-to-income ratio and asset-liability ratio, rural households face a heavier burden of debts than urban households. 10.5 % of all indebted rural households are in insolvency and have high financial risks. From a regional perspective, a larger proportion of western rural households have high financial risks than the eastern and central regions. These high financial risk households mainly have large debts, low incomes, and low assets; the debts are mainly for production, business operation, education, and medical services. The debt risk index refers to a certain household group's proportion of risky debts. If insolvency serves as the standard for financial risk, 9.6 % of rural households' debts are risky debts. Since most rural households' debts are from private loans, however, risky debts have thus farhadlittle impact on the banking system.

8.1 Overview for Financial Risks

8.1.1 Debt Burden for Rural Households

As shown in Chart 8.1, among all surveyed households, 33.9 % are indebted, but the proportion for rural households is 37.7 and 3.8 % higher than the overall level. Although the proportion is higher, the scale of rural household debts is not as high. According to 2013 CHFS, only 15.8 % of the total debt comes from rural households. The debt per household for all indebted households was 134,745 Yuan while the number was 55,113 Yuan for rural households, far lower than the overall amount.

L. Gan et al., *Report on the Development of Household Finance in Rural China (2014)*, DOI 10.1007/978-981-10-0409-4_8

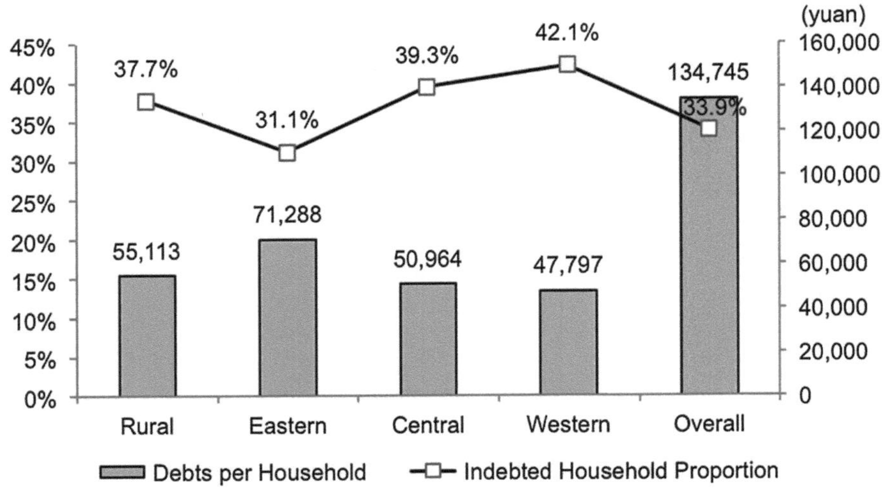

Chart 8.1 Indebted proportion and debts scale of rural households

From a regional perspective, the proportion of indebted households in the eastern, central, and western regions are 31.1, 39.3, and 42.1 %, respectively, with the western region ranking the highest and the eastern ranking the lowest. Indebted households have 71,288 Yuan, 50,964 Yuan, and 47,797 Yuan in debt in the eastern, central, and western regions, respectively. In comparison, rural households in the eastern region have the highest debt level while western rural households have the lowest.

In general, households with low incomes are more likely to take out a loan, but their financial capacity is also lower. Due to the income disparity between the urban and rural areas, rural households have a naturally higher indebted proportion, but their income level constrains their ability to take out loans. As a result, the scale of rural households' debts is far lower than the overall level. According to the CHFS data, in 2012, the after-tax household incomes of rural households in the eastern, central and western regions were 41,786 Yuan, 35,046 Yuan, and 33,183 Yuan, respectively, with the eastern region ranking the highest and the western region ranking the lowest. Consequently, the western region has the highest proportion of indebted households but lowest scale of debts.

8.1.2 Definition and Measurements of Household Financial Risks

Household financial risks, namely the default risk of household debts, refer to the possibility of causing the lender a certain amount of loss when the borrower (household) fails to repay the principal and interest in a timely and accurate manner.

Household financial risks are related to households' repayment ability; this means that households with stronger repayment abilities have lower financial risks. In household finance, the capital for repaying debts comes mainly from household income or selling assets. Therefore, this report reflects the debt repayment ability of households with two indexes and further illustrates the size of household financial risks.

$$\text{Financial Risk Index I} = \text{Debts}/\text{After} - \text{tax Income}$$

$$\text{Financial Risk Index II} = \text{Debts}/\text{Assets}$$

Financial Risk Index I measures the amount of household debts relative to after-tax income, namely the year that households need to check in and return all of their debts with current after-tax income and debt level. The larger the debt-to-income ratio is, the weaker the household's repayment ability is and the higher its financial risks are.

Besides repaying debts with income cash flow, under some circumstances, households can also acquire capital to repay their debts by selling assets. As a result, the debts-to-assets ratio, namely the asset-liability ratio, can also be used to measure household financial risks. The higher the household's debts-to-assets ratio is, the weaker its repayment ability and the higher financial risks are.

In this report, we regard insolvent households as households with high financial risks their overall debts have exceeded their assets and they bear such a heavy debt burden that they cannot repay it all by selling assets.

8.1.3 Household Financial Risk Level

As shown in Table 8.1, of the research samples all households, 33.9 % of households face debt burdens, with a debt-to-income ratio of 197.8 %, meaning that their debts are nearly twice as much as their after-tax incomes. In rural research samples, 37.7 % of households have credit and debt-to-income ratios of 155.0 %, meaning

Table 8.1 Debt-to-income ratio and asset-liability ratio of households in China (*unit* %)

	Overall	Rural
All samples		
Debt-to-income ratio	68.7	59.1
Debt-to-income ratio (house mortgage loans excluded)	42.5	47.9
Asset-liability ratio	5.9	6.8
Indebted samples		
Debt-to-income ratio	197.8	155.0
Debt-to-income ratio (house mortgage loans excluded)	113.0	131.4
Asset-liability ratio	15.8	16.6

Table 8.2 Debt-to-income ratio and asset-liability ratio of households in China and the U.S. (*unit %*)

	China (2012)	China rural (2012)	U.S. (2007)	U.S. (2010)
All samples				
Debt-to-income ratio	68.7	59.1	84	90
Asset-liability ratio	5.9	6.8	14.8	16.4
Indebted samples				
Debt-to-income ratio	197.8	155.0	149	166
Asset-liability ratio	15.8	16.6	19.4	22

(*Source* of U.S. Data) Changes in U.S. Family Finances from 2007–2010: Evidence from the Survey of Consumer Financers (R/OL); Board of Governors of the Federal Reserve System, www.federalreserve.gov

that their debts are nearly 1.6 times their incomes and lower than the overall level. Judging from the asset-liability ratio, the ratio for all indebted households is 15.8 %; for rural indebted households that figure is slightly higher, reaching 16.6 %.

House mortgage loans are considered to be medium and long term credit. Thus, borrowers can divide them into several parts and repay them successively over a long period of time. If house mortgage loans are excluded, the debt-to-income ratio of rural households is 47.9 % and the debt-to-income ratio of indebted rural households is 131.4 %, both of which are higher than the overall level. This shows that, compared with urban households, rural households still have a heavier debt burden.

Table 8.2 also compares the debt-to-income ratio and asset-liability ratio for households in the United States. Generally speaking, both Chinese household ratios are lower than those of the United States in 2007 and 2010. For indebted Chinese households, however, their debt-to-income ratio exceeds that of the United States. Also, although indebted rural households in China have a lower debt-to-income ratio than the overall Chinese level, the ratio is approximately that of households in the United States. Hence, it is noteworthy that households in China (including rural households) already face a relatively heavy debt burden.

From a regional perspective, there is little difference in financial risks in rural households in the eastern, central, and western regions if measured by the debt-to-income index; the debt-to-income ratios reach 156.6, 155.8, and 152.5 %, respectively. The asset-liability ratio for central rural households, however, is relatively higher, reaching 19.0 %; this is 3.3 and 3.4 % higher than eastern and western rural households (See Chart 8.2).

8.1.4 Characteristics of High-Financial Risk Households

This report defines insolvent households as high-financial-risk households. As shown in Chart 8.3, 8.1 % of overall indebted households are in insolvency and the proportion surges to 10.5 % for rural indebted households (2.4 % higher than the

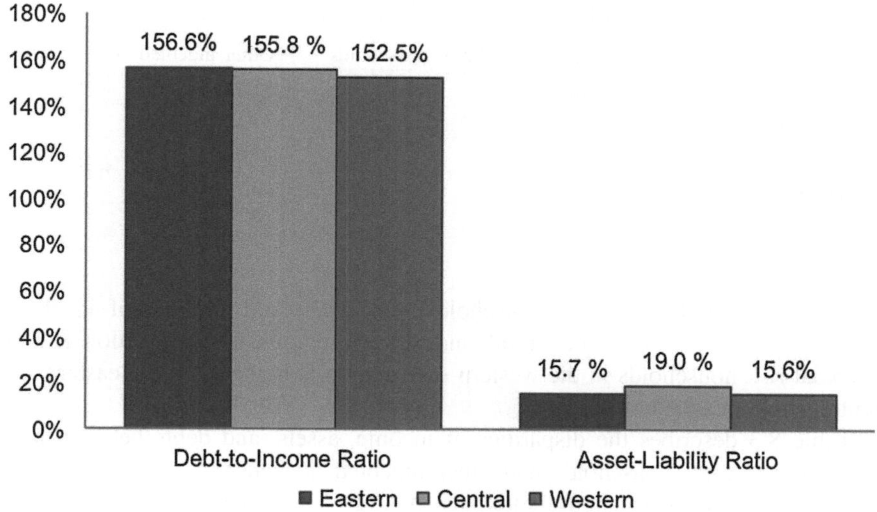

Chart 8.2 Financial risk indexes for chinese indebted households in eastern, cenral and western regions

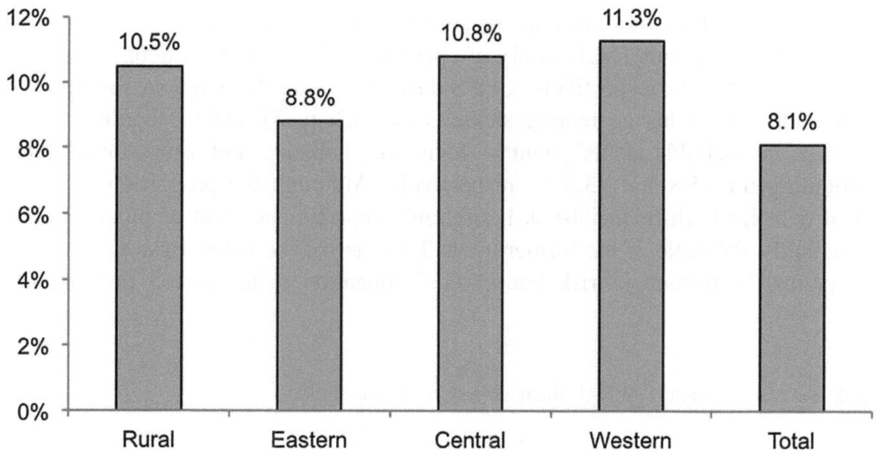

Chart 8.3 The proportion of high-financial-risk households in indebted households

overall level). CHFS data shows that, among all the surveyed rural household samples, 4.0 % of them have negative net assets. The proportion is relatively high. The proportion of households that successfully filed for bankruptcy in the United States[1] was only 1, 1.3, and 1.4 % in 2008, 2009, and 2010, respectively.

[1]Please refer to www.usacourts.gov and www.census.gov.

Table 8.3 Debt burdens of high-financial-risk rural households (*unit* Yuan)

	High-financial-risk households	Other indebted households
Debts per household	97,828	51,489
Asset per household	46,753	370,904
Income per household	19,939	37,584
Asset-liability ratio (%)	209.2	13.9
Debt-to-income ratio	4.9	1.5

Of China's indebted rural households, 8.8, 10.8, and 11.3 % of insolvent households are in the eastern, central, and western regions. The proportion of high financial-risk households in the western rural region is higher than the eastern and central rural areas.

Table 8.3 describes the disparities of income, assets, and debts between high financial-risk rural households and other indebted households. As shown in the table, high-financial-risk households have 97,828 Yuan in debt, nearly twice of other indebted households. Assets per household, however, are only 46,753 Yuan, far lower than other indebted households (assets per households are 370,904 Yuan). The asset-liability ratio of high-financial-risk households is 209.2 %, with a debt-to-income ratio which is 4.9 times higher.

As shown in Table 8.4, from the perspective of debt structure, high-financial risk household debt is comprised mainly of operational debt and other debt, accounting for 36.2 and 30.4 %, respectively. CHFS data shows that the major reason for other rural household debts is treating sickness (see Chap. 5). On the contrary, other indebted households debts' mainly focus on housing and operational debts, accounting for 45.8 and 33.0 %, respectively. Although the proportion of operational debt for high-financial-risk households approximates that of other indebted households, the scale of the former totals 2.1 times of the latter. Besides, data also shows that high-financial-risk households' education debts exceed that of other

Table 8.4 Debt structure of high-financial-risk rural households

	High-financial-risk households		Other indebted households	
	Mean (Yuan)	Proportion (%)	Mean (Yuan)	Proportion (%)
Agricultural/industrial and business debts	35,449	36.2	16,997	33.0
Housing debts	16,143	16.5	23,598	45.8
Automobile debts	2464	2.7	32,797	6.4
Education debts	13,333	13.6	2033	3.9
Credit card debts	634	0.6	1093	0.2
Other debts	29,804	30.4	5473	10.7
Total debts	97,828	100.0	51,489	100.0

indebted households both in proportion and in scale, 80 % of which is obtained from private channels.

In conclusion, high-financial-risk rural households are mainly households with high debts, low incomes, and low assets. They take out loans mainly for production and operation, education, and curing diseases.

8.2 Debt Risk Index

8.2.1 Definition of Debt Risk Index

Debt risk index refers to the ratio that embodies a household's risky debts which lies in 0–1. For example, if the index is 50 %, the proportion of the household's risky debts of total debts is 50 %. The larger the index is, the larger the proportion of risky debts is.

The debt risk index's advantage lies in the fact that it can comprehensively measure a household's risky debt and take both the financial risk level of every household and the impact of debt size imposed on total debt risk into consideration.

8.2.2 The Construction of the Debt Risk Index

The formula of debt risk index is as follows:

$$\mathrm{Index} = \frac{D_{risk}}{D} = \frac{\sum_{1-1}^{1-m} P_i D_i}{D}$$

Pi refers to the debt risk coefficient of household i, Di refers to the debt balance of household i, and D refers to the total debts of all households.

The basic idea of the debt risk index is: ① first, estimate each household's debt risk coefficient Pi; ② multiply the debt risk coefficient Pi by the household's debt Di, and we can get the each household's amount of risky debt; ③ add every household's risky debt and we can get the total amount of risk debt of all households D_{risk}; ④ divide the total amount of debts by the total amount of risky household debt to get the risk debt ratio (a household's debt risk index).

The key step of the above process is estimating the debt risk coefficient Pi of each household; therefore, we attempt to set up a Probit model:

$$\Pr(Y|X) = \alpha + \beta X$$

Y = 1 means that the debt is risky while Y = 0 means that the debt is not risky. Insolvency is the standard for verifying the level of a household's debts level of risk; X is a range of factors that affect debt risk, including consumption and

Table 8.5 Debt risk index of overall and rural households (*unit* %)

	Rural	Eastern rural	Central rural	Western rural	Overall
Indebted households	37.7	31.1	39.3	42.1	33.9
Debts per indebted households (Yuan)	55,113	71,288	50,964	47,797	134,745
Financial risk index	9.6	9.8	10.0	9.1	6.5

expenditures, years of education, household registration status, employment status, marital status and household size, etc.[2]

8.2.3 *Debt Risk Index Level*

Table 8.5 shows the debt risk index of indebted rural and overall households. The debt risk index for all in debted households is 6.5 % and the debt risk index of indebted rural households is 9.6 and 3.1 % higher than all households. This means that if insolvency is used to measure risk, 9.6 % of the total debts of rural households are risky debts. The data shows that although the debt per indebted rural household is lower than the overall level, indebted rural households still have a heavy debt burden and the proportion of their risk debts is relatively high. From a regional perspective, the debt per indebted rural household in the eastern region (71,288 Yuan) is higher than that in the central and western regions. Taking the debt risk index as the measurement, households in eastern China do not have higher debt risk.

From the perspective of risky debt proportion, the debt risk is not low in rural households. Since most rural household debts come from private lending (see Chap. 9), risk debt has little impact on the banking system.

8.3 Financial Risk of Different Households

8.3.1 *Household Income and Financial Risk*

As shown in Table 8.6, from the perspective of the different income levels of rural households, the proportion of indebted low-income households is relatively low, accounting for only 4.7 %. They have heavy debt burdens however, as the debts per household are 52,185 Yuan, 16,007 Yuan and 5578 Yuan higher than that of

[2]See the selection of variables in the research of Danial and Monica (2007), Sobehart and Keenan (2002), and Herrala and Kanla (2007).

Table 8.6 Financial risk of indebted rural households with different income levels (*unit* %)

Income level	Proportion of indebted households	Debts per household (Yuan)	Proportion of households in insolvency	Risk index
Low-income	34.7	52,185	14.9	11.5
Lower-middle-income	38.1	36,178	12.7	10.6
Upper-middle-income	39.7	47,607	10.7	9.6
High-income	38.1	83,784	5.7	8.3

lower-middle-income households and upper-middle-income households. 38.1 % of high-income households are indebted. This approximate slower-middle-income households and upper-middle-income households, but their debts per household (83,784 Yuan) rank the highest. This suggests that, from the perspective of household income levels, the debt levels of indebted households present a U-shaped structure and low-income and high-income households have relatively heavy debts.

The proportion of insolvency in low-income households is as high as 14.9 % while the proportion in higher-income households is relatively lower (5.7 %). Measured by the debt risk index, the proportion of risk debts of low-income households is also the highest. The debt risk index of rural high-income, upper-middle-income, lower-middle-income, and low-income households are 8.3, 9.6, 10.6, and 11.5 %, respectively.

8.3.2 Age Structure and Financial Risk

Table 8.7 shows that households with ahead of household below the age of 29 comprise the highest proportion of indebted households (47.8 %) followed by

Table 8.7 Financial risk of indebted rural households with different age levels (*unit* %)

Age level	Proportion of indebted households	Debts per household (Yuan)	Debt-to-income ratio	Risk index
Below 29 years old	47.8	56,735	130.8	8.9
30–39 years old	40.2	56,103	183.1	8.0
40–49 years old	45.1	64,309	171.4	9.4
50–59 years old	37.6	54,458	166.4	10.2
Above 60 years old	22.3	47,743	151.6	12.2

Table 8.8 Financial risk of indebted rural households with different educational backgrounds (*unit %*)

Education background	Proportion of indebted households	Debts per household (Yuan)	Debt-to-income ratio	Risk index
Primary school or lower	30.6	44,923	155.0	11.9
Junior secondary school	38.1	57,365	143.1	9.9
Senior secondary, Technical school	40.4	74,065	186.8	11.5
Junior college or higher	50.5	88,191	155.4	8.3

households with ahead of household between the ages of 40–49 (45.1 %). The proportion of indebted households with a head of household over the age of 50 ranks the lowest and the size of their debts is also lower than the young and middle-aged households.

From the perspective of debt-to-income ratio, households with ahead of household between the ages of 30–39 have the heaviest debt burdens and their debt-to-income ratio is 183.1 %. Using the debt risk index as the unit of measurement, senior households have the highest debt risk and 12.2 % of their debts are risky debts.

8.3.3 Education Background and Financial Risk

Table 8.8 shows that the more educated a household is, the more indebted the household is. Indebted households with ahead of household that has a primary school education or lower have the lowest amounts of risky debt, accounting for 30.6 %. 50.5 % of indebted households with ahead of household with a junior college education or higher have risky debt. The debt per household of indebted rural households with the head of households' education background of junior college or above is 88,191 Yuan, much higher than other households. From the debt risk index perspective, the proportion of households with ahead of household with a primary school education or lower or senior high school/vocational school educations or higher that have riskiest debt are the highest at 11.9 and 11.5 %, respectively. Those with less education have more risk.

Chapter 9
Rural Households' Private Lending

Lending behavior among rural households is an important part of the rural financial market, not only promoting households' income levels but also eliminating rural poverty and narrowing income disparity. In the rural areas, due to serious information asymmetry in the lending market, the informal financial market is an effective complement to the formal financial market. In 2013, 40 % of rural households participate in private lending; this proportion is far higher than the overall level. Private lending funds are mainly used for housing and production and operation, however, the funds mainly come from siblings and other relatives and friends. Only a small proportion of households obtain loans from informal financial organizations.

9.1 Participation Rate in Private Lending

In this chapter, private lending refers to the loans that an individual obtains from sources other than financial institutions like banks or credit cooperatives. The loans come from parents and relatives, friends and colleagues, and informal financial organizations. Due to serious information asymmetry existing in the lending market, the informal financial market is an effective complement to the formal financial market. Particularly in the rural areas, it is difficult for banks to obtain information about the loan repayment ability of potential lenders; thus, the method of private lending meets the demand of most rural households. Lending behaviors among rural households arean important part of the rural financial market, not only promoting the households' income level but reducing rural poverty and narrowing the wealth gap.[1]

[1]See the research of Khandker (1988).

L. Gan et al., *Report on the Development of Household Finance in Rural China (2014)*, DOI 10.1007/978-981-10-0409-4_9

Table 9.1 Participation rate of private lending (*unit* %)

Region	Participation rate of private lending
Overall	34.7
Rural	43.8

Table 9.2 Participation rate of different private lending (*unit* %)

	Agriculture/business	Housing	Automobile	Education
Overall	9.2	21.2	2.2	5.9
Rural	14.5	25.7	2.1	8.6

The participation rate in private lending refers to the proportion of households which hold private loans. As Table 9.1 shows, 34.7 % of all households participated in private lending in 2013, and the participation rate of rural households was 43.8 %. This suggests that there is a booming private lending activity among rural households in China which resembles the findings of other domestic and foreign scholars.

Table 9.2 shows the participation rate of private lending households in agriculture/business, housing, automobiles, and education. As shown in Table 9.2, 21.2 % of all households hold private lending for purchasing or constructing houses, 9.2 % have them for agriculture/business production and operation, 5.9 % for education, and 2.2 % for purchasing automobiles. In rural households, 25.7 % have private loans for purchasing or constructing houses, 14.5 % for agriculture/business production and operation, 8.6 % for education, and 2.1 % for purchasing automobile. Above all, Chinese households, particularly rural households, participate more in housing and agriculture/business production and operations.

9.2 Scale of Private Lending

The scale of private lending refers to the amount of private lending funds that remain unpaid by households. Table 9.3 illustrates the 2013 private lending scale per household. From Table 9.3 we can see that the private lending scale per

Table 9.3 Scale of private lending (*unit* Yuan)

Region	Private lending	Proportion of private lending in total debts (%)
Rural	36,500	64.6
Eastern region	46,600	64.7
Central region	38,100	71.5
Western region	28,100	57.4
Overall	41,500	32.0

Table 9.4 Different purposes for private lending

	Agriculture/business	Housing	Automobiles	Education
Private lending (Yuan)	11,000	13,100	2000	2400
Proportion of private lending in total debts (%)	58.1	57.5	63.0	72.8

household of rural households is 36,500 Yuan and private lending accounted for 64.6 % of all debts. The private lending scale per household of rural households in the eastern region is 46,600 Yuan and private lending accounts for 64.7 % of the total debt. The private lending scale per household of rural households in the central region is 38,100 Yuan and private lending accounts for 71.5 % of the total debt. The private lending scale per household of rural households in the western region is 48,100 Yuan and the private lending accounts for 57.4 % of the total debts. The overall private lending scale per household is 41,500 Yuan and private lending accounts for 32.0 % of total debts. The data shows that the private lending scale of rural households is not large, but the proportion of private lending in their total debt is higher than the overall level. This suggests that rural households' loans were obtained primarily from private lending. This is particularly prominent in rural households in the central region.

Table 9.4 illustrates the scale of private lending for different purposes. From Table 9.4 we can see that the mean value of private loans that rural households have for agriculture and business operation is 11,000 Yuan, accounting for 58.1 % of all production and operation debts. The mean value of the private loans that rural households have for housing is 13,100 Yuan, accounts for 57.5 % of total housing debts. The mean value of private lending of rural households hold for purchasing automobiles is 2000 yuan, accounting for 63.0 % of total automobile debts. The mean value of private lending of rural households hold for education is 2400 Yuan, accounting for 72.8 % of all education debts. From the above data we find that the scale of private lending of households hold for housing is the largest. In addition, the proportion of private lending rural households hold for education in total debts is the highest, which shows that rural households' loans are mainly obtained from private lending.

9.3 Sources of Private Lending

In the CHFS questionnaire, the sources of households' private lending are divided into six categories: parents, children, siblings, other relatives, friends/colleagues and informal financial organizations. Table 9.5 shows the proportion of private loans that households obtain from parents, children, siblings, other relatives, friends/colleagues and informal financial organizations. 32.0 % of all households obtained funds from siblings. Brothers and sisters were the main sources of private

Table 9.5 Sources of private lending (*unit* %)

Area	Parents	Children	Siblings
Rural	3.5	4.2	36.1
Urban	7.7	1.2	28.1
Overall	5.6	2.7	32.0
Area	Other relatives	Friends/colleagues	Informal financial organization
Rural	30.4	18.4	0.7
Urban	21.8	14.8	0.5
Overall	26.1	16.6	0.6

lending followed by other relatives, then friends. Only a small proportion of households obtained loans from informal financial organizations.

In rural areas, siblings are the main source of private lending, the proportion of which is 36.1 %. 30.4 % of rural households obtain loans from other relatives, and only 0.7 % get loans from informal organizations. This suggests that Chinese households emphasize relationships. Rural households, in particular, prefer to borrow from relatives.

9.4 Purposes of Private Lending

In the CHFS questionnaire, the purposes of private lending capital are categorized as follows: agriculture/business operation, constructing or purchasing housing, purchasing automobiles, education, and others. Table 9.6 shows the proportions of all the purposes of private lending.

In the overall country, the proportion of private lending for constructing or purchasing houses ranks the highest and 40.6 % of all households' loans are used for housing. This is followed by private lending used for agriculture/business operation; 31.8 % of overall households' borrowing is used for this. In contrast, the proportion of households' private lending used for purchasing automobiles and education is small, accounting for 4.2 and 3.8 %, respectively.

In rural areas, 34.9 % of rural households' loans is used on houses. Mean while, 32.4 % of households' private lending is used for agriculture/business. These two constitute the major reasons for rural households' private lending.

Table 9.6 Purposes of private lending (*unit* %)

	Agriculture/business	Housing	Automobile	Education	Others
Overall	32.4	34.9	3.6	4.7	24.4
Rural	31.8	40.6	4.2	3.8	19.6

Chapter 10
Financial Knowledge of Rural Households

In order to better understand the financial knowledge of households in China as well as study how this knowledge influences households' financial and economic behaviors, a series of questions on financial knowledge was designed in the second round of 2013 CHFS to measure Chinese households' financial knowledge.[1] Based on the answers to these questions, we have used factor analysis to calculate the financial knowledge index.

While analyzing the financial knowledge of Chinese households, we discovered that Chinese households generally lack financial knowledge and there is a significant disparity between the regions and between the urban and the rural areas. The study also discovered that education greatly influences financial knowledge, and economic and financial training courses, in particular, are highly influential. In researching the financial behaviors of households with different financial knowledge, we realize that households with more financial knowledge have higher participation rates in financial markets, and possess more risky assets. The more financial knowledge households possess, the more likely it is that they will obtain loans and the less likely it is they will participate in private finance. In addition, financial knowledge also greatly affects household consumption. A higher proportion of households with more financial knowledge use debit cards, credit cards, and online shopping. Consequently, households' financial knowledge greatly affects their economic behavior in various aspects. With China's generally low financial knowledge and the great disparity between regions and between the urban and the rural areas, however, households in China (especially in the western region

[1]Guiso and Jappelli (2008) find in their research that it is wrong to measure the interviewee's financial knowledge simply by asking them how they know about finance (a.k.a. their objective financial knowledge). Because over-confident investors tend to overestimate their financial knowledge while passive investors are more likely to underestimate. As a result, compared with objective financial knowledge, financial knowledge index of questionnaires designed for financial knowledge of investors can reflect their financial knowledge in a more accurate way.

L. Gan et al., *Report on the Development of Household Finance in Rural China (2014)*, DOI 10.1007/978-981-10-0409-4_10

Table 10.1 Answers to questions on interests and calculation abilities (*unit %*)

		Correct	Incorrect	Don't know
China	Overall	14.1	33.4	52.5
	Urban	16.7	40.0	43.4
	Rural	10.6	24.4	65.0
Holland		76.2	19.6	3.8
U.S.		67.1	22.2	9.4

and the rural areas) need improved financial knowledge in order to enhance their participation in economic activities and promote economic growth.

10.1 Integral Level of Financial Knowledge

10.1.1 Answers to Financial Knowledge Questions

10.1.1.1 Question on Interest and Calculation Abilities

Question: Imagine that you have 100 Yuan and the bank's annual interest rate is 4 %. What is the total amount of capital and interest you will receive in 5 years if you make a fixed deposit?

1. Less than 120 Yuan
2. 120 Yuan
3. More than 120 Yuan
4. I don't know.

Table 10.1 illustrates that 14.1 % of households answer correctly while those who "Don't know" account for as much as 52.5 % on a simple question of calculating interest. The proportions of households answering correctly in Holland and the U.S. are 72.6 and 67.1 %, respectively, while households answering "Don't Know" in the two countries account for only 3.8 and 9.4 %.[2] As a result, China's households lack the basic ability to calculate a deposit interest rate. The problem is more prevalent in the rural areas. Only 10.6 % of rural households in China answered the question correctly while 65 % of rural households had no idea about the answer. Thus, though the majority of Chinese households deposit their money, they have little understanding about calculating interest.

[2]The data of Holland is calculated on the basis of DHS (the DNB Household Survey) by Rooij and other people in 2011. Data of the U.S. is calculated by Lusardi and Mitchell in 2011, based on HRS (Health Retirement Survey) in the U.S. in 2004.

Table 10.2 Answers to question on inflation (*unit* %)

		Correct	Incorrect	Don't know
China	Overall	15.6	40.6	43.7
	Urban	16.0	49.7	34.3
	Rural	15.2	28.3	56.5
Holland		82.6	8.6	8.5
U.S.		75.2	13.4	9.9

10.1.1.2 Question on Inflation

Question: Imagine that you have 100 Yuan and the bank's annual interest rate is 5 % with an annual inflation rate of 3 %. After leaving a deposit of 100 Yuan in the bank for a year, how many things can you buy with the amount of money you receive from the bank?

1. More than one year ago
2. As many as one year ago
3. Less than one year ago
4. I don't know.

As shown in Table 10.2, the proportions of households in China that answered the question correctly, incorrectly, and "I don't know" are 15.6, 40.6, and 43.7 %, respectively. It is also clear that far more households in Holland and the U.S. answered correctly than in China, reaching 82.6 and 75.2 %, respectively. On this question, rural households' accuracy is similar to that of the overall level but the proportion of rural households answering "I don't know" is much higher than the overall level. It can thus be concluded that the majority of rural households have no knowledge of inflation.

10.1.1.3 Question on Financial Market Risks

Question: In your opinion, is it more risky to purchase stock from one company than purchase an equity fund?

1. Yes
2. No
3. I've never heard of stocks before.
4. I've never heard of equity funds before.
5. I've never heard of either of them before.

As shown in Table 10.3, the proportions of Chinese households answering correctly and incorrectly are 26.9 and 21.8 %, respectively. The accuracy of answers to the financial market risk question is higher than the question on interest calculation and inflation, but the proportion of households answering "I don't know" was also 51.3 %. Thus, households with better knowledge of financial

Table 10.3 Answers to question on financial market risks (*unit* %)

		Correct	Incorrect	Don't know
China	Overall	26.9	21.8	51.3
	Urban	38.0	24.0	38.0
	Rural	11.8	18.9	69.3
Holland		48.2	24.8	26.6
U.S.		52.3	13.2	33.7

markets answer with higher accuracy and the low accuracy is generally due to alack of knowledge about financial risk markets. Approximately 51.3 % of overall households have no knowledge of financial risk markets. Households in developed countries such as Holland and the U.S., however, are much less likely to answer "I don't know" than households in China. From a domestic perspective, there is a great disparity between the urban and rural areas. The proportion of rural households answering correctly and "I don't know" are 11.8 and 69.3 %, respectively. All of above shows that rural households are in great need of knowledge about financial markets.

10.1.1.4 Question on Attention to Economy and Finance

Question: How often do you follow economic and financial information in your daily life?

1. Always
2. Frequently
3. Occasionally
4. Rarely
5. Never

As shown in Table 10.4, judging from their answers on attention to economic and financial programs, only 11.4 % of all households pay much attention to economic and financial issues, while 64.6 % of households pay little to these issues in their daily lives. As a result, the low accuracy of answers to the above three questions is due to alack of financial knowledge. In addition, compared with households from developed countries, the disparity of the financial knowledge of households in our country is huge. Meanwhile, households in the urban and the rural areas perform significantly differently on answering financial questions.

Table 10.4 Attention to economy and finance (*unit* %)

	Much	Regular	Little
Overall	11.4	24.0	64.6
Urban	12.2	27.7	60.1
Rural	10.5	18.9	70.6

In conclusion, the proportion of Chinese households that are able to answer economic and financial questions correctly is far lower than in developed countries in Europe and the United States. The majority of households in China answered the questions with "I don't know" because they lack financial knowledge. Additionally, the disparity of households' answers between the urban and rural areas is significant, showing that there is a great gap in financial knowledge.

10.1.2 The Construction of the Financial Knowledge Index

To more accurately measure various households' levels of financial knowledge, we attempt to make a score based on their answers to the questions. On such a basis, we adopt factor analysis[3] to construct the financial knowledge index in order to measure each household's financial knowledge. We divide the answers to the above four questions into seven smaller questions by dividing each of the three of them (excluding the question on attention to the economy and finance) into two smaller questions. One of the two smaller questions refers to whether the households have answered the question directly, thereby defining the answer "I don't know" as an indirect answer and marking as 0, while marking the opposite as 1. It is generally believed that households answering "I don't know" have a significantly different level of financial knowledge than those answering directly. This is because the answer "I don't know" may indicate that the household has no understanding of the question while a wrong answer may be caused by superficial understanding. The other smaller question refers to the accuracy of direct answers, marking a correct answer as 1 and an incorrect one as 0. It is obvious that households that answer the questions correctly have better financial knowledge than those answering incorrectly.

10.1.2.1 Factor Analysis

Table 10.5 illustrates the factor loading of the analysis of these questions. The result of factor analysis shows that there are six common factors. The larger the factor loading is, the stronger the explanation provided by the factors on the questions is. Judging from the loading of the factors, factors 1, 2, and 3 are of larger loading coefficients. Since the major concern is households' financial knowledge, it is more important to find out the factors influencing the financial knowledge.

The factor loading of all the factors shows that factor 1 has a positive influence on all the answers to the questions. In other words, factor 1 will enhance households' attention to economic and financial programs as well as improve the

---

[3]Please refer to the studies partially done by Lusardi in 2011 and the studies partially done by Rooij in 2011.

Table 10.5 Factor loadings

Questions	Answers	Factor 1	Factor 2	Factor 3	Factor 4	Factor 5	Factor 6
Pay attention to economic and financial information or not	Pay attention to economic and financial information	0.212	−0.012	0.056	0.076	0.194	0.015
Answer questions concerning interest calculation or not	Directly answered	0.765	0.321	−0.246	−0.081	0.057	−0.051
Answers to questions concerning interest calculation	Correct	0.377	0.234	−0.328	0.168	−0.066	−0.051
Answer questions concerning inflation or not	Directly answered	0.746	0.285	0.262	−0.126	−0.044	0.037
Answers to questions concerning inflation	Correct	0.319	0.214	0.353	0.182	−0.020	−0.030
Answer questions concerning financial market risk or not	Directly answered	0.669	−0.471	−0.006	0.007	0.003	0.089
Answers to questions concerning financial market risk	Correct	0.609	−0.488	−0.008	0.024	−0.037	−0.092

directness and accuracy of the households' answers to economic and financial questions. As a result, it is reasonable to believe that factor 1 reflects households' abilities to correctly answer financial questions, namely their financial knowledge. Next, we will measure the specific financial knowledge of households by computing factor scores.

10.1.2.2 Calculating Factor Scores

The factor scores of households regarding factor 1 is calculated according to the ratio of factor scores and the answers to the questions (illustrated in Table 10.6).

Table 10.6 The ratio of Factor 1 score

Questions	The ratio of Factor 1 score
Pay attention to economic and financial information or not	0.032
Answer questions concerning interest calculation or not	0.362
Answers to questions concerning interest calculation	0.073
Answer questions concerning inflation or not	0.317
Answers to questions concerning inflation	0.067
Answer questions concerning financial market risk or not	0.269
Answers to questions concerning financial market risk	0.210

Equation (10.1) offers the way to calculate the factor scores:

$$\text{Factor\_score}_1 = \sum\nolimits_{1-1}^{7} \beta_{1n} Q_{!x} \qquad (10.1)$$

Each household's factor scores can be calculated by using Eq. (10.1) with each household's answers and the ratio of factor score. In order to more directly reflect household financial literacy and standardize each household's factor scores, this report introduces Eq. (10.2) to standardize this procedure.

$$\text{Index\_Finance} = \frac{\text{Factor Score}_1\ \mathit{Min}(\text{Factor Score}_1)}{\mathit{Max}(\text{Factor Score}_1)\ \mathit{Min}(\text{Factor Score}_1)} \qquad (10.2)$$

The standardized index is the index of financial literacy which reflects household financial literacy. This index range is from 1 to 100. 0 stands for households of the lowest financial literacy while 100 stands for households with the highest financial literacy. Table 10.7 illustrates the distribution of household financial literacy.

As is illustrated in Table 10.7, more than 20 % of the households score 0, indicating that those households either gave wrong answers or no answers to relevant questions. It can be inferred that there's a huge discrepancy in China's household financial literacy.

10.1.3 Financial Literacy

10.1.3.1 Overall Household Financial Literacy

As is illustrated in Chart 10.1, the overall financial literacy of Chinese households scored 42.0. The figures for the United States and the Netherlands are 75.3 and 78.8, respectively, by the same calculation method. The overall financial literacy of Chinese households lags far behind developed countries in Europe and the United States. Only the 20 % of Chinese households with the highest household financial literacy meet the average level of European countries and the United States.

Table 10.7 The distribution of household financial literacy

	Quantile 10	Quantile 20	Quantile 30	Quantile 40	Quantile 50	Quantile 60	Quantile 70	Quantile 80	Quantile 90
Household financial literacy	0	0	20.2	27.2	44.1	56.1	64.9	76.7	89.5

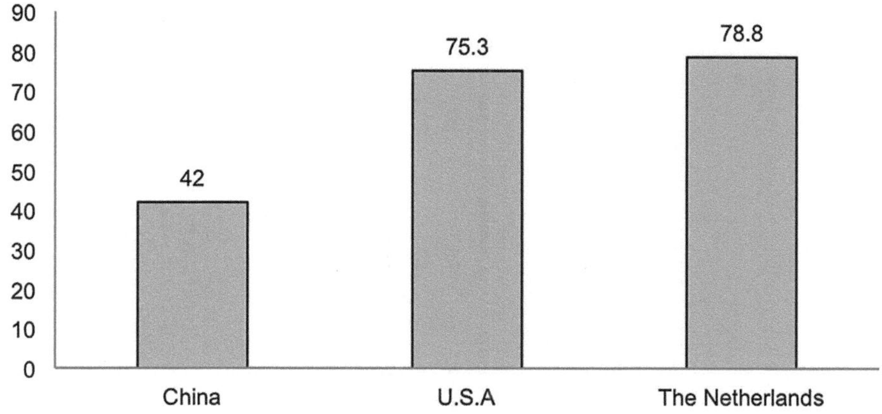

Chart 10.1 A comparison of financial literacy between China and countries in Europe and the United States

10.1.3.2 The Gap Between Urban Households and Rural Households in China in Terms of Financial Literacy

There's a huge gap between urban and rural households in China. The average urban household's financial literacy score is 51.4 while the average rural household financial literacy score is only 29.4. It can be inferred that rural households in China manifestly lack financial knowledge as is shown in Chart 10.2.

As is shown in Table 10.8, approximately 40 % of rural households scored 0 on their financial literacy while the figure is 20 % for urban households. In terms of each quantile, rural household financial literacy lags behind that of urban households.

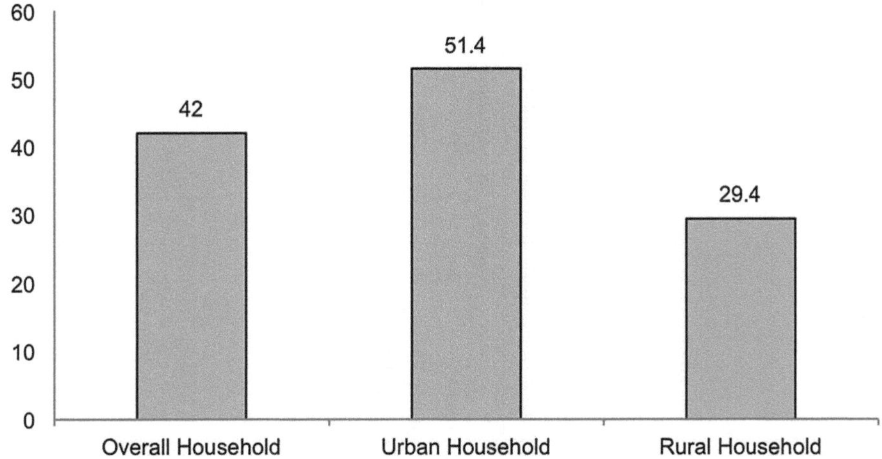

Chart 10.2 Financial literacy of households in China

Table 10.8 A comparison of the financial literacy of urban and rural households

	Quantile 10	Quantile 20	Quantile 30	Quantile 40	Quantile 50	Quantile 60	Quantile 70	Quantile 80	Quantile 90
Nationwide	0	0	20.2	27.2	44.1	56.1	64.9	76.7	89.5
Urban population	0	20.2	27.2	46.5	56.1	68.7	76.7	87.1	92.1
Rural population	0	0	0	2.4	23.9	31.3	51.1	56.5	76.3

Table 10.9 A comparison of household financial literacy of households in the eastern, central, and western regions

	Eastern region	Central region	Western region
Nationwide	47.6	42.4	40.3
Urban households	53.3	51.1	49.3
Rural households	29.6	30.8	27.5

10.1.3.3 Regional Discrepancies in Household Financial Literacy in China

In terms of regional discrepancy, households in the eastern score 44.1, ranking the first among all the three regions, followed by households in the central region which score 42.7 while households in the western region score 38.7, ranking the last of the three regions. It can be inferred that there is a positive correlation between household financial literacy and economic development. Household financial literacy scores were higher in more economically developed regions. One noteworthy thing is that rural households in the central region score higher than rural households in the eastern region as is shown in Table 10.9.

10.2 The Distribution of Financial Literacy

This section discusses the distribution of financial literacy in terms of demographic features like level of education, age, and gender.

10.2.1 The Relationship Between Educational Level and Financial Literacy

As is shown in Chart 10.3, in terms of financial literacy, urban illiterate households score 13.2 while rural illiterate households score 11.4. Urban households with secondary senior school educations score 55 while rural households with secondary senior school educations score 45.2. It can be concluded that there is a strong connection between educational level and financial literacy. The higher the level of education is, the higher the household's financial literacy score is.

As is shown in Chart 10.4, households with economic and financial educational backgrounds score 74.4 for financial literacy while households without such educational backgrounds score 39.6.

It is the same for rural households in that rural households with economic and financial educational backgrounds score 59.8, higher than the 28.8 that rural

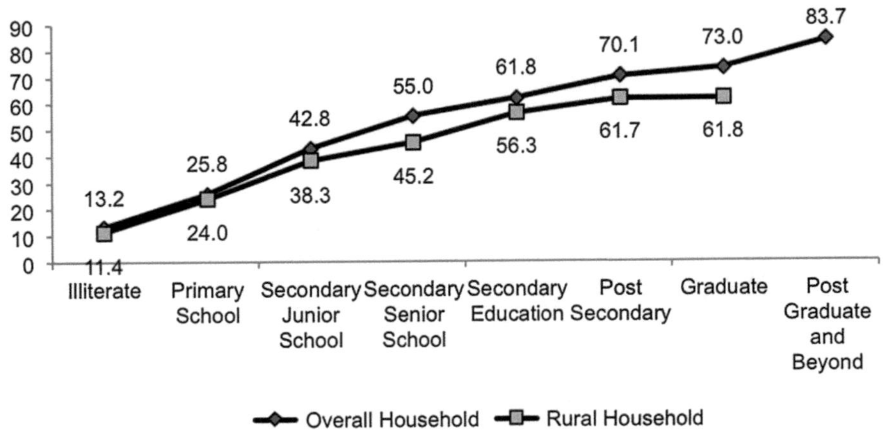

Chart 10.3 Financial literacy of people of different years of education

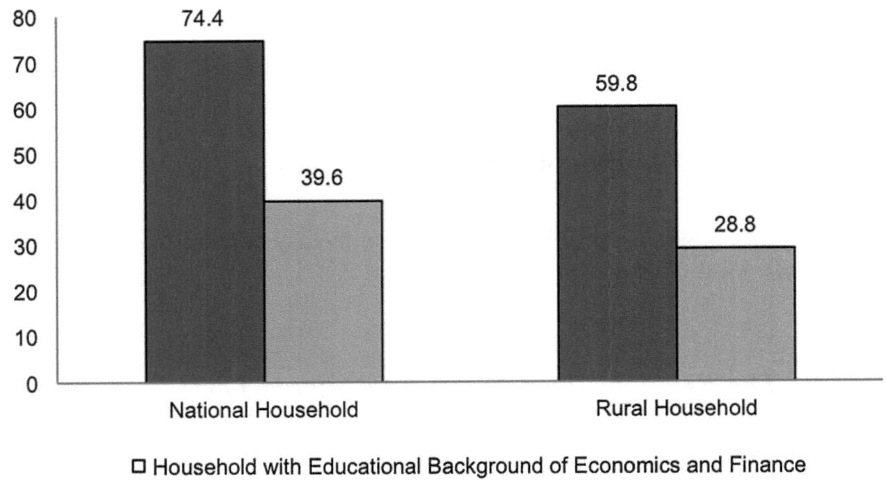

Chart 10.4 Educational background of economics and finance's influence on household financial literacy

households without such educational backgrounds. Having an economic and financial educational background significantly improves household financial literacy.

As is illustrated in Chart 10.5, economic and financial courses have a greater impact on households with low levels of education, indicating that financial courses more effectively improve the financial literacy of households with low levels of education.

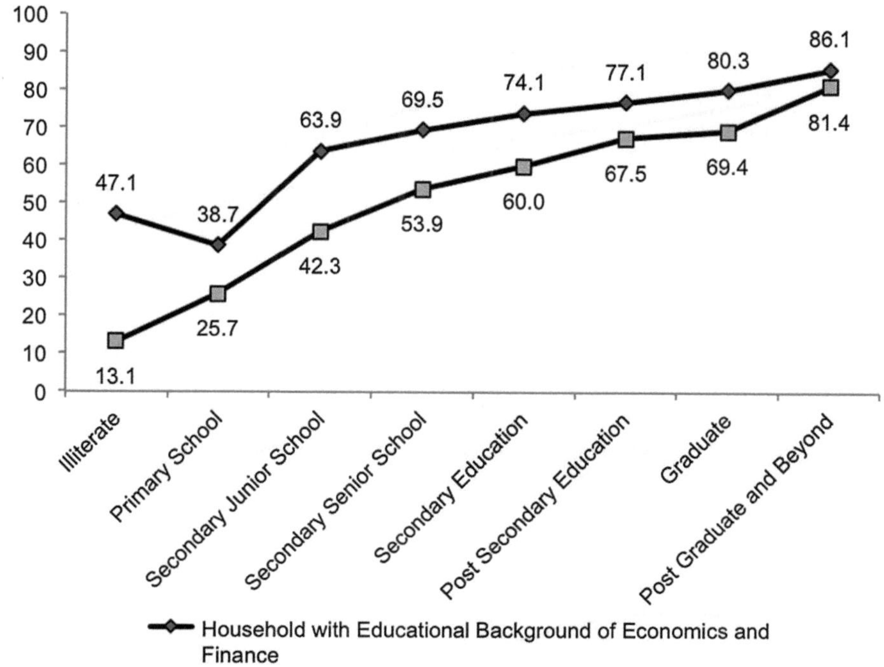

Chart 10.5 Educational background of economics and finance's influence on different educational levels

10.2.2 *The Relationship Between Age and Financial Literacy*

As is shown in Chart 10.6, people between the ages of 16 and 20 (not including 20) score 62.5 on their financial literacy tests; the figure is 51 for the rural population. People who are at least 60 years old score 28.6 for their financial literacy; the figure is 19.2 for the rural population. It can be inferred that younger people score higher for their financial literacy both in the rural areas and nationwide.

As shown in Chart 10.7, the reason why younger people score higher on financial literacy is because they receive higher levels of education. Thus, this report draws the conclusion that the discrepancy between age groups regarding financial literacy is due to differences in the number of years of education.

10.2.3 *The Relationship Between Gender and Financial Literacy*

As is illustrated in Table 10.10, male financial literacy is slightly higher than female financial literacy nationwide; in the rural areas, male financial literacy is

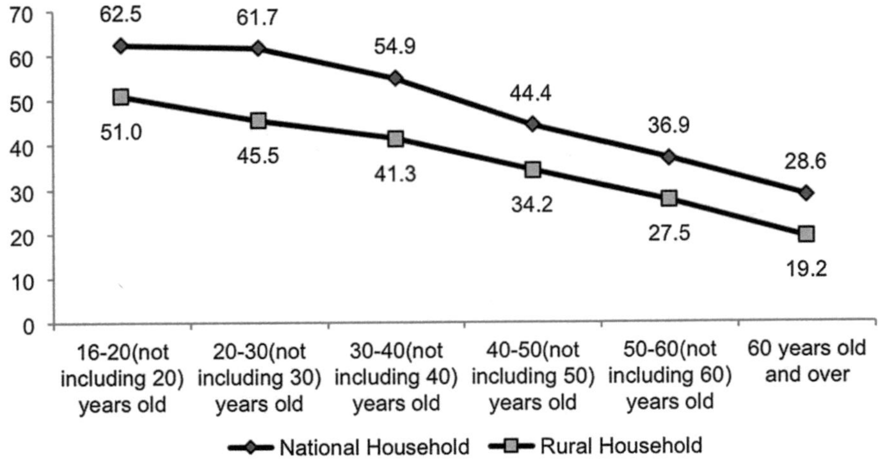

Chart 10.6 Financial literacy of different age groups

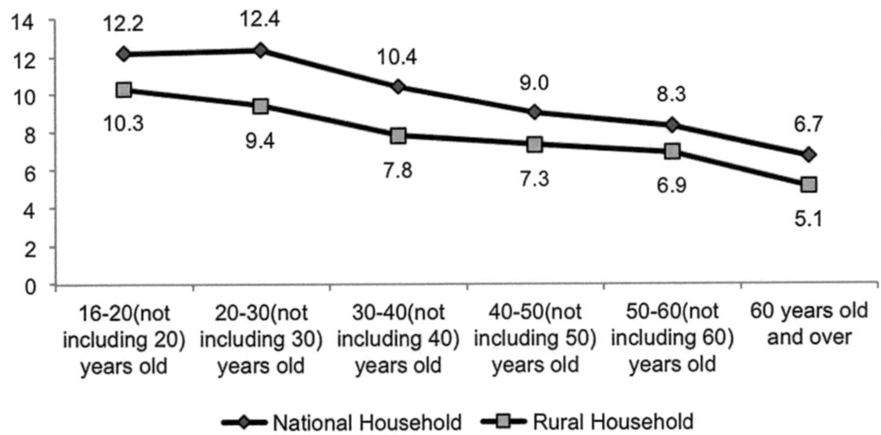

Chart 10.7 Different years of education of different age groups

Table 10.10 Financial literacy of different gender group

	Financial literacy (Index)		Years of education (Years)	
	Overall household	Rural household	Overall household	Rural household
Male	42.5	31.6	9.1	7.4
Female	41.5	25.8	8.4	5.6

significantly higher than female financial literacy. The same is true regarding the level of education. Nationwide, males receive slightly more years of education than females while in the rural areas males receive far more years of education than female. The discrepancy between the genders' levels of financial literacy is due to differences in the years of education they receive.

Thus, it can be inferred that improved educational levels will lead to improved household financial literacy. In the meantime, especially for households with low levels of educational, receiving financial training can help significantly improve household financial literacy.

10.3 The Relationship Between Financial Literacy and Household Financial Behaviors

10.3.1 Influence on Participation in Financial Market

Chart 10.8 illustrates how financial literacy affects household participation in the financial market. Household participation in the financial market refers to household participation in risky markets such as the stock market, fund market, bond market, and household possession of financial products, derivatives, and gold.

As is illustrated in Chart 10.8, of the nation's 20 % most financially illiterate households, only 0.9 % participates in the financial market and this figure is 0.4 % in the rural areas. Of the nation's 20 % most financially literate households, 31.1 % participate in the financial market and the figure is 5.9 % in the rural areas. The higher a household scores regarding its financial literacy, the more it participates in the financial market.

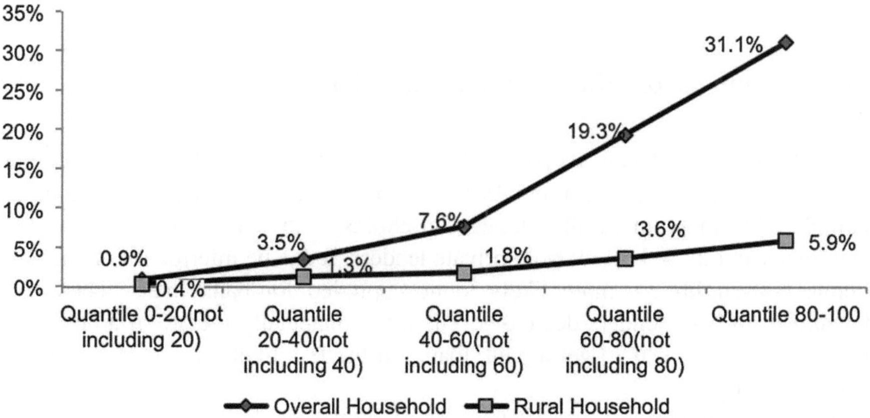

Chart 10.8 Impact of financial literacy on household participation in financial market

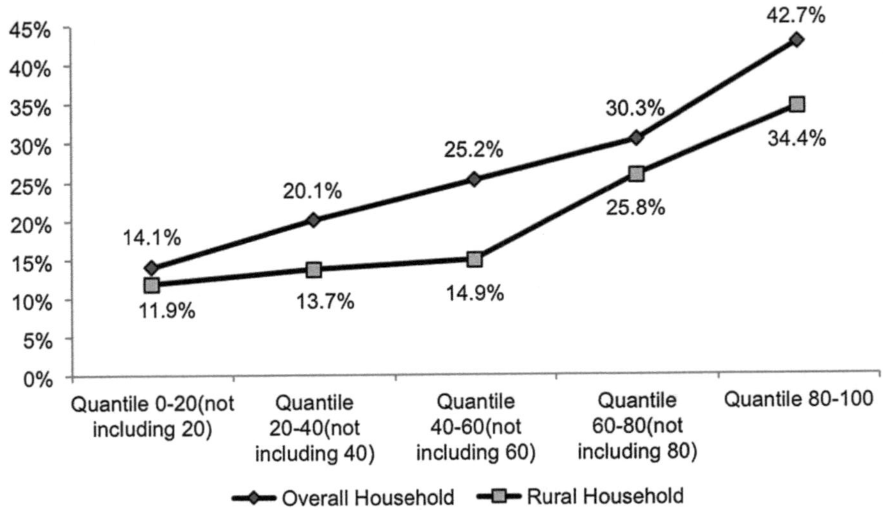

Chart 10.9 Financial literacy and the ratio of risk assets

10.3.2 Impact on Risky Asset Allocation

As is illustrated in Chart 10.9, of the nation's 20 % most financially illiterate households, 14.1 % own risky assets and the figure is 11.9 % in the rural areas. Of the nation's 20 % most financially literate households, 42.7 % own risky assets and the figure is 34.4 % in rural areas. Households with higher levels of financial literacy are more likely to own risky assets.

10.3.3 Impact on Household Credit Behavior

As is illustrated in Chart 10.10, of the nation's 20 % most financially illiterate households, 10.4 % owe debt and 38.5 % borrow from private lenders. Among the nation's 20 % most financially literate households, 23.5 % have been approved for bank loans and 27 % borrow from private lenders. It can be inferred that financially literate households are more likely to be approved for bank loans. Thus, their demand for private lenders decreases. The more financially literate of a household is, the more likely it is to get a bank loan and the less likely it is to participate in private lending.

As for the impact of financial literacy on rural household credit behavior, the same pattern is observed the more financially literate a household is, the more likely it is to receive a bank loan. As is illustrated in Chart 10.11, of the nation's 20 %

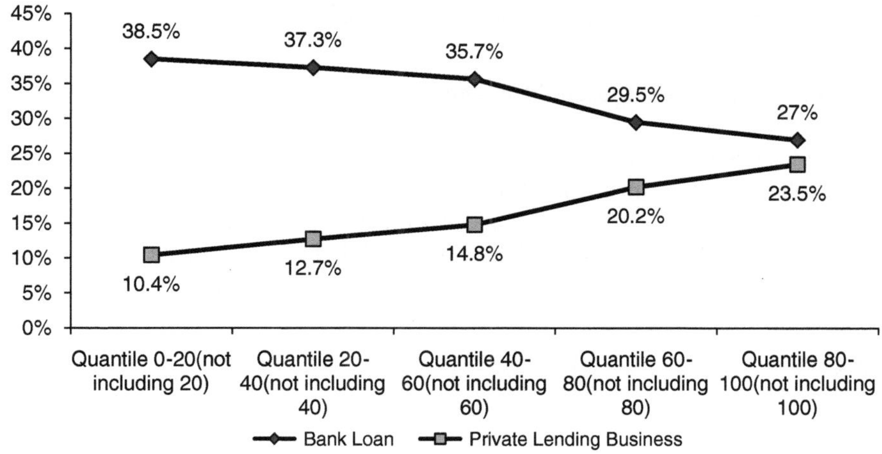

Chart 10.10 Financial literacy and household loans (Nationwide)

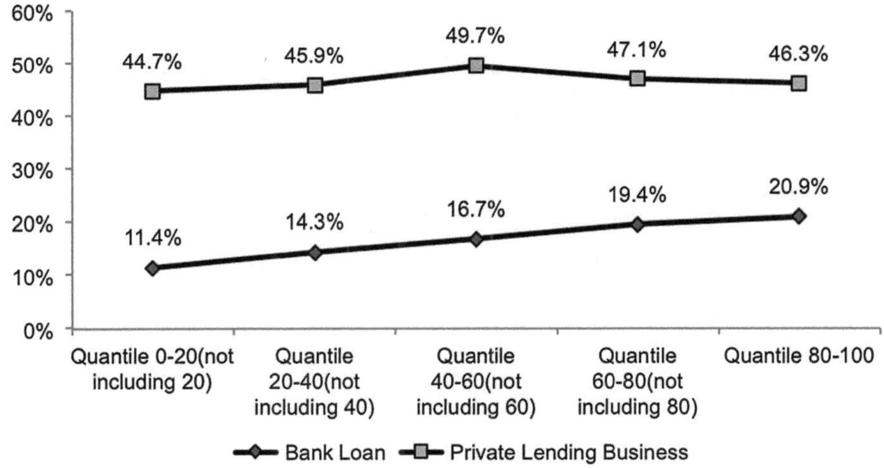

Chart 10.11 Financial literacy and households loan (Rural area)

most financially illiterate households, 11.4 % of them received loans from banks. Of the nation's 20 % most financially literate rural households, 20.9 % received loans from banks. In conclusion, financial literacy has no obvious impact on rural household's participation in private lending which might result from social ties between rural households.

10.3.4 Impact on Household Consumption

10.3.4.1 Impact on Household Payment Methods

As is illustrated in Chart 10.12, of the nation's 20 % most financially illiterate households, 1.5 % of them use debit cards and the figure is 0.9 % for rural households. Of the nation's 20 % most financially literate households, 23.9 % of them use debit cards and the figure is 6.6 % for rural households. Thus, it can be concluded that more financially literate households tend to use debit cards more often.

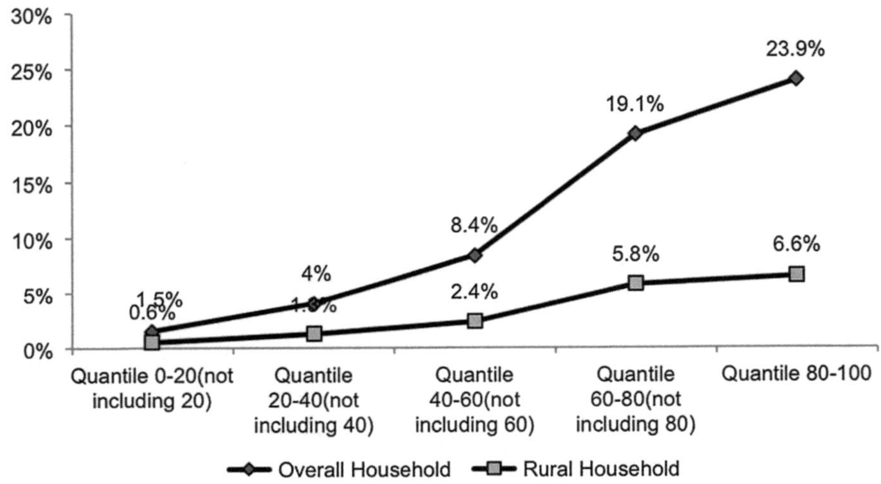

Chart 10.12 Financial literacy and household debit card usage

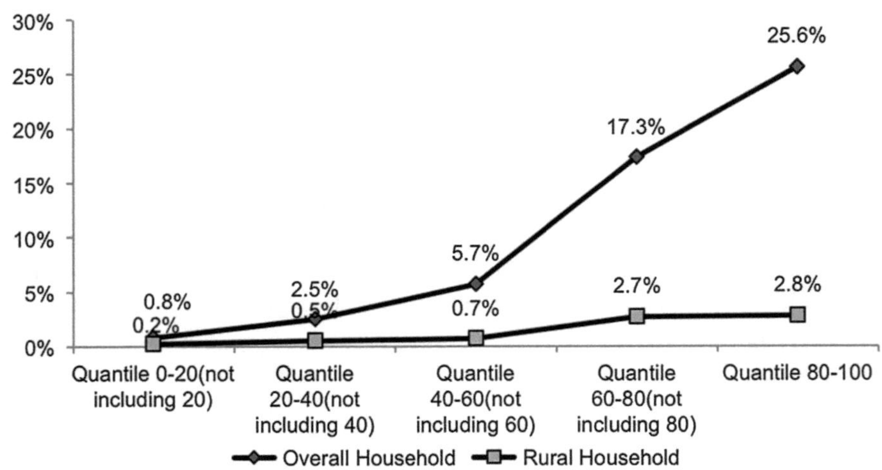

Chart 10.13 Financial literacy and household credit card usage

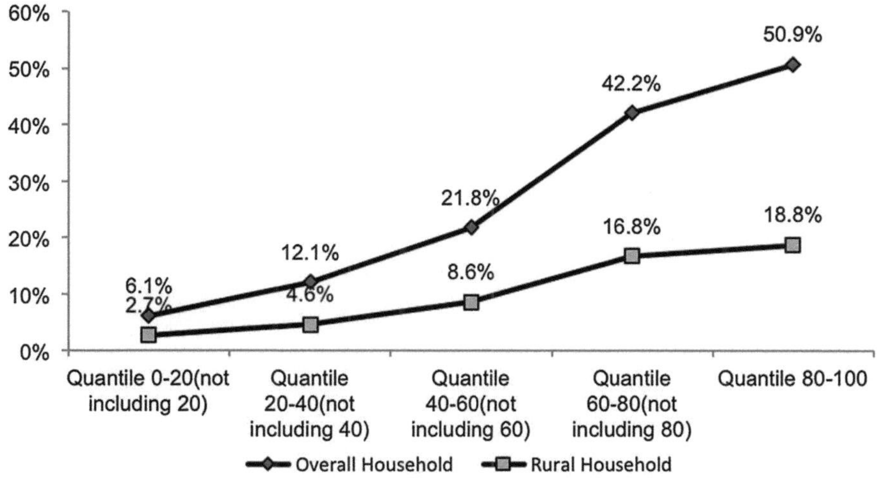

Chart 10.14 The impact of financial literacy on household online shopping

As is illustrated in Chart 10.13, of the nation's 20 % most financially illiterate households, 0.8 % of them use credit cards and the figure for rural households is 0.2 %. Among the nation's 20 % most financially literate households, 25.6 % of them use credit cards and the figure is 2.8 % for rural households. Thus, it can be concluded that more financially literate households are more likely to use credit cards.

10.3.4.2 Impact on Household Online Shopping

As is illustrated in Chart 10.14, of the nation's 20 % most financially illiterate households, 6.1 % of them shop online and 7.7 % of rural households do. Among the nation's 20 % most financially literate households, 50.9 % of them shop online and the figure is 18.8 % for rural households. Thus, it can be concluded that more financially literate households are more likely to shop online.

MIX
Papier aus verantwortungsvollen Quellen
Paper from responsible sources
FSC® C105338

If you have any concerns about our products,
you can contact us on
ProductSafety@springernature.com

In case Publisher is established outside the EU,
the EU authorized representative is:
Springer Nature Customer Service Center GmbH
Europaplatz 3, 69115 Heidelberg, Germany

Printed by Libri Plureos GmbH
in Hamburg, Germany